THE VOYAGES OF DISCOVERY

THIS IS THE STORY of man's exploration of the earth's oceans and islands from earliest times to modern age. The book opens with a study of the ancient mariners of the Mediterranean cultures, and traces how a growing body of knowledge, especially Phoenician, passed down through Greece and Rome to the medieval European world, menaced and shut in as it was at first by the Ottoman threat.

With the dawning of the Renaissance, however, a profound change is seen. The work of scientists and humanists, doubting whether the earth was really flat, or the heart of the universe, encouraged the thought of men like Prince Henry the Navigator of Portugal, and the voyages of men like Vasco da Gama and Christopher Columbus. After illustrating the struggle for control of the New World, the book examines the discoveries made by Le Maine, Schouten, Tasman, Le Bruyn, Cook and others in Australasia, and looks particularly at Cook's unique achievement in charting much of the Pacific Ocean for the first time. The history of cosmography is completed by the adventures of Drake, Hawkins, Frobisher, Hudson, Ross, Scott, and others in the Arctic and Antarctic—the last great areas charted by man. A final chapter treats a topic seldom illustrated at much length—the science of navigation, dealing not only with maps but with compasses, sextants, chronometers, and other aids.

A PUTNAM PICTORIAL SOURCES BOOK

THE VOYAGES
OF
DISCOVERY

Edited by
G. R. CRONE

Research by
ALAN KENDALL

G. P. PUTNAM'S SONS · NEW YORK

The Putnam Pictorial Sources Series

Frontispiece: Captain James Cook

Copyright © 1970 by Wayland (Publishers) Ltd
All rights reserved. This book, or parts thereof, must not be
reproduced in any form without permission
Published simultaneously in the Dominion of Canada by
Longmans Canada Limited, Toronto

Library of Congress Catalog Card Number: 70-116157

Printed in England

CONTENTS

CHAPTER ONE

NEW HORIZONS

By G. R. Crone, MA, FRGS

THE VOYAGES OF DISCOVERY illustrated in this book were the first phase of a great outward movement of peoples from Europe which carried, especially in the nineteenth century, millions of migrants to new homes across the oceans. As a result of this expansion, Europe ceased to be a group of peninsulas and islands on the edge of the known world, and became for centuries the focus of power in international affairs, and the leader in commerce and industry. Although today this control has passed into the hands of other and more powerful nations, the influence of Europe is still significant, for these migrants carried with them not only their language, but also their political institutions, their culture, and their religion. Where they arrived as settlers on a large scale, they founded communities which grew to nationhood, politically independent of their homelands. The greater part of the North American population is of European stock, and shares a common cultural inheritance; the same is true of Australia and New Zealand. In South America, Iberian and indigenous elements have combined to produce distinctive "Latin American" cultures. In Asia, the impact has been less pronounced—mainly because the first European pioneers came into contact with great populations with ancient and stable civilizations.

Nevertheless, in Asia the results of this confrontation have been important. The example of Japan is, perhaps, the most striking; here, Western ideas and technologies have been adopted on a large scale. In India, where they arrived in the first place as traders and conquerors, one-seventh of the world's population is striving to strengthen and develop a democratic and industrialized society on Western lines. For long periods, China has isolated herself from the outside world. Yet she, too, has adopted Western technology, and uses political theories first evolved in the West. Undoubtedly, Europe today no longer exercises so much influence, but to speak of "the decline of the West" is only half the truth.

These epoch-making discoveries were achieved by tough, courageous seamen and traders—men often fanatical in their determination. Their stories are notable not only because of the events they foreshadow; they are records of the age-long struggle of man against the forces of nature, and of his continued efforts to reveal and understand the world around him. We must, of course, study more prosaic matters, such as shipbuilding, navigation, commodities, and money. But in doing so we should not overlook this adventure of the human spirit.

These pioneers were admittedly often ruthless toward their defeated enemies— perhaps no less so than when they were fighting wars in Europe. They made mistakes, too, some of which still plague the world today. Yet, on occasion, they could rise above meaner considerations.

Their adventures, recorded for example in the writings of Richard Hakluyt and Samuel Purchas, have fascinated generations of readers. Selected from contemporary sources, the illustrations which follow help us to see what manner of men they were, the ships they sailed, and something of the lands and peoples they saw.

This "oceanic age," or age of the great discoveries, lasted approximately from A.D. 1400 to the early nineteenth century. This, at least, was the European age of discovery, when the peoples of western Europe broke out from the Mediterranean onto the high seas. Earlier civilizations, too, had sent out explorers and traders to lands beyond their own bounds. In the early centuries of our era, the Chinese, for example, had journeyed throughout central and southern Asia, and were active on the seas. In the fourteenth century, their ships were sailing to southern India and the Persian Gulf. But none of them pursued exploration so extensively and determinedly as the new nations of maritime Europe. What struck the people of Ceylon when the first Portuguese arrived, was their amazing energy and restless activity.

For southeast Europe, Asia, and the Mediterranean, the earliest voyagers of which we have details were the Egyptians. The Egyptians may have been the first to move from river navigation to the open sea. Our story opens with them. As with most early peoples, their motive was mainly to extend their commerce. In the course of time, they and their successors —Phoenicians, Greeks, and Romans— developed a type of craft adapted to conditions in the enclosed and tideless Mediterranean. This was the galley, a long, relatively narrow vessel which relied on manpower, usually provided by slaves

at the oars supplemented by a sail on a single mast. With this type of vessel, the Phoenician Hanno is believed to have reached as far as West Africa. The Greek Pytheas sailed from the Greek colony of Marseilles through the Strait of Gibraltar to Britain, and beyond to the Island of Thule. He may even have reached Iceland or the Norwegian coast. In Graeco-Roman times, there was also a flourishing trade from Egyptian ports on the Red Sea across the Indian Ocean to southern India. It is possible that some traders continued farther eastward to the Golden Chersonesus (the Malay Peninsula).

Following the decline of Roman power, western Europe engaged in the political and social reconstruction which led to the emergence of the new nation states of the Renaissance. Harassed by the Vikings, and dangerously threatened by the advance of Islam in the southeast, her attention was turned inward. Contacts with the outer world were infrequent and spasmodic. With the growth of order and stability, however, a lively domestic maritime commerce grew up. The Italian city states, especially Pisa, Venice, and Genoa, were in the forefront. They extended their trading activities to the eastern Mediterranean and the Black Sea, and westward along the Atlantic coast to England and the rising cities of Flanders. Seaborne trade was often safer than that which went overland. There was less disturbance from wars, fewer taxes and tolls, and less loss through brigandage. An armed merchant ship carried its own protective force. No land power, however, would welcome a strong armed merchant convoy crossing its territory.

Through these centuries, the nations of the Iberian Peninsula—Spain and Portugal—were expanding their mercantile fleets and seeking new markets, mostly outside the Mediterranean. They were rapidly followed by France, England, and the Hanseatic League. With all this activity, there developed a new type of ship specially built to navigate the waters of the North Atlantic, and to carry cargoes of greater bulk. These were stoutly built sailing ships, able to negotiate conditions for which the Mediterranean galley was unsuited. Methods of navigation on the high seas also evolved. In the Mediterranean, it had rarely been necessary to observe the stars for latitude. In the waters of the Atlantic, the pioneers learned the expertise which enabled them eventually to reach the Indies and to circumnavigate the globe. The Atlantic gave them long experience of battling with weather, tides and currents, and shoal water, and of planning the best course to steer. They learned through constant readiness to meet an unexpected emergency, and through toughness to endure the frightening hardships of life on a long voyage.

Meanwhile, in the Indian Ocean, the trade in Eastern spices and luxuries which the Greeks and Romans had organized, continued. But it did so in different hands —those of the Persian and Arab seamen, who extended it to the Eastern islands and the ports of southern China. At Alexandria and Cairo these wares were purchased by Venetian merchants at an exorbitant price, and distributed by them throughout Europe. Sometimes interrupted but never completely ended, this traffic was dominated by the Egyptian Mamelukes and, later, by the Ottoman Turks. Eventually, the Portuguese diverted most of it to the Cape of Good Hope route.

The lead in this expansion beyond European waters was taken by the small country of Portugal. Conveniently placed on the Atlantic seaboard beyond the Strait of Gibraltar, and obliged through lack of resources to seek a livelihood from the sea, she had for centuries looked southward to the African coasts which promised a harvest of food and a profitable trade. This was but one expression of the growing intellectual, political, and economic activity which reached new heights with the Renaissance. Engaged in a bitter struggle with the Ottoman Turks, the Mediterranean rulers sought possible allies among African and Asian potentates. The Church, alarmed at the shrinking frontiers of Christendom, sought compensation by carrying the Faith to distant heathen peoples. The rulers and the great commercial houses hoped the Tropics would yield up gold, precious stones, spices, and drugs which would stimulate their economies and satisfy their lust for national power, at the expense of the despised— yet hated—infidels. But embracing all these trends was that general spirit of intellectual curiosity and the search for new knowledge which we know as the Renaissance. Delving into the newly discovered works of ancient Greek and Roman authors, scholars and scientists speculated on where land and water lay upon the surface of the globe. They sought for clues to the fabled lands of which they read, formulated problems for the explorers to solve, and were eager to suggest how they should begin work.

The main problem which engaged the cosmographers (world geographers) was: What does the unknown half of the globe contain? We are reminded of the space astronauts in recent times: No one had ever actually seen the reverse side of the moon, yet it was presumed to exist before their own voyage of circumnavigation finally revealed it. The Florentine scientist,

Paolo Toscanelli, underestimated the distances involved in the earth's surface, and argued that the other half of the surface would simply prove to be a continuation of the Asian continent and islands eastward.

Directed by Prince Henry the Navigator, Portuguese sea captains began the long, and at first slow, voyaging southward which brought them at last to India, to the Golden Chersonesus of the ancients, and ultimately to China and Japan. These efforts were rewarded by control of the coveted spice trade. Earlier in the decade in which Vasco da Gama sailed his fleet to the Indian port of Calecut, Christopher Columbus also sought "the Indies" by sailing in the opposite direction, westward from the Canary Islands. What he found in October, 1492, was not the land of the Great Khan as he expected, but the Islands of the Caribbean. Not until Ferdinand Magellan crossed the Southern Pacific to the Philippines, did the Spaniards reach the Spice (Molucca) Islands.

For a century, the Portuguese were masters of the Oriental trade, until, following political events in Europe, this passed in the seventeenth century to the Dutch and the English. It was the Dutch commander, Abel Tasman, who established that Australia was a great island, and not part of the supposed "great southern continent," and who landed on the coast of New Zealand. The last phase of oceanic development was mainly confined to the Pacific and Polar regions. British, French, Russian, and American explorers revealed the immensity of the Pacific, charted its manifold island groups, and determined the outlines of the Antarctic continent. Thus, by the year 1850 the coastlines of the continents had been explored and for the most part charted.

The explorers had greatly extended the horizons of Western man. In doing so, they confirmed the theories of the classical authors in some respects, proving, for example, that the earth was a sphere. In other respects, they showed that older opinions were unsound. Contrary to the views of some early writers, including Claudius Ptolemy, the oceans in all zones were navigable, and the "Sea of India" was not landlocked. So the authority of the ancient writers was gradually demolished. Men reasoned more profoundly and systematically from their own observations about the nature of the world and its inhabitants, to relate cause and effect. In widening the outlook, the explorers had thus contributed significantly to the evolution of modern scientific thought. At first they had, understandably, regarded the strange new world under the influence of ideas of their own time. In the illustrations to the collections of travels, the explorers of America sometimes appear in the guise of medieval knights, and there is often more than a touch of a Roman Senator about eighteenth-century Pacific chiefs. With the development of the scientific outlook, the study of native peoples became more serious. The scientists who sailed with the expeditions made extensive collections of botanical and zoological specimens, and of the tools, utensils, clothing, and arms of primitive peoples. It was some time, however, before they abandoned the current romantic style in their landscapes and seascapes. This deeper understanding of other lands and their peoples was the work of the successors to the pioneers: men whom we might call explorers rather than discoverers. The world owes a great debt to those who have "adventured their persons to find out the true circuit thereof."

Although we know from Sumerian and Akkadian inscriptions of the third millennium B.C. that maritime relations existed between Mesopotamia and the lands bordering the Persian Gulf, it is the Egyptians who provide us with one of the earliest documented sea-going expeditions. Egyptian ships ventured into the Mediterranean, the Red Sea, and the Indian Ocean, and toward the end of the fifteenth century B.C., Queen Hatshepsut sent a fleet to Punt, generally identified as the Somali coast of Africa opposite Arabia. There had been previous expeditions to Punt, so Hatshepsut's was not, strictly speaking, a voyage of discovery—except in its motive.

Early Egyptian boats had no keels, so if a boat was riding the waves, all the weight was concentrated in the beam. The beam was the only part of the boat actually in the water. The boat could, and apparently did, sometimes

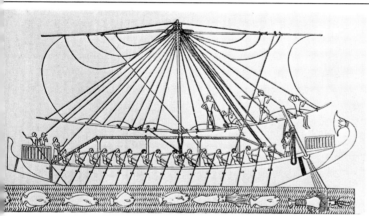

1

2

3

break in two. To counteract this, a twisted rope was fastened from one end of the boat to the other, as can be seen in the drawing from the temple at Deir-el-Bahri of one of Hatshepsut's ships (1), and the model reconstructed from it (2). Note also the two spars lashed together near the mast to form the yards above and below the sail, and the double-oar system for steering (3, 4). The mast on earlier Egyptian ships consisted of two pieces of wood erected in an inverted V (5), though later the single mast was adopted, largely under the influence of the Phoenicians.

The ancient Egyptians believed that the human soul, after the death of the body, followed the sun in his endless voyage across the world. They therefore frequently buried a model boat or ship close to the corpse, manned by a crew of model people as in this funerary boat from Thebes (6).

4

5

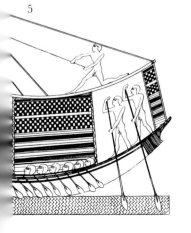

6

Despite their achievements, the Egyptians were not great sailors, compared with the Phoenicians and Greeks. The Phoenicians introduced keels and developed the astronomical science of Babylon to which they had access. Later the Greeks took this to a new level at Alexandria, whose great lighthouse was one of the seven wonders of the world. This engraving (7) is from John Harris's *Voyages* (London, 1764). The founder of Alexandria, Alexander the Great (356–323 B.C.), was planning a voyage of discovery to the coasts of Arabia at the time of his death. His death delayed the inauguration of Greek commerce with India for two centuries, but the fact that the Greeks reached India at all is a telling tribute to their seamanship. Greek ships were generally single-masted (8, 9) with a

7 8

9

single sail which was used when the wind was fair. The principal means of moving the ship along, however, was by oars. For the merchant ships, capacity was more important than speed, but the warships were fast and streamlined (8, 9, and 10). Note also the beak or ram on the prow of these ships and the oars for steering (11). A rudder as such on the stern was a much later development. Much confusion has been caused by the fact that the Greeks called their their major warships *trieres* (*triremes* in Latin) (12), and much energy has been devoted to working out how ships with several banks of oars could be made to function. One of the latest theories put forward is that the oars were on two levels, but that the rowers sat three abreast. This has a great deal to commend it, especially as *quinqueremes* are also mentioned.

13

10

11

12

Around the time of Greek development in seamanship, symbolized on this sixth-century vase (13), the Phoenicians were covering more and more of the Mediterranean and began to put their skills at the disposal of other peoples. We read in the Bible (1 Kings 9:26) how Hiram, King of Tyre, a Phoenician, built ships for King Solomon at Ezion-geber on the Red Sea. Phoenician ships were also used by Sennacherib, King of Assyria, as can be seen in the relief from his palace at Nineveh (14). The presence of armed men and the beaked prow show that this must be a warship. The boats in use for general transportation were much more humble affairs. In (15) bricks to build the Palace of Sennacherib are being moved along the River Tigris by boat, and men are fishing from inflated animal skins.

Initially Phoenician skill at sailing developed because their trade developed. However, as

13

14

they sailed farther and farther away from their homeland in the eastern Mediterranean, it became necessary to establish outposts. It must be remembered that at this time, sailing was still a question of going from headland to headland, and that mariners seldom ventured out into the open sea. The Phoenicians, however, were more daring than most, and it seems likely that they even ventured through the Strait of Gibraltar and up to Britain. One of the Phoenician outposts, Carthage, on the coast of North Africa, became a great power in the political sense, and challenged the might of Rome. The struggle is depicted in mosaics at Ostia (16, 17). In fact, it was as a result of the threat from Carthage that Rome came to have a Navy at all, with ships like these (18) shown in mosaics from the same place. One Carthaginian, Hanno, is even thought to have navigated as far as the Gulf of Guinea.

In 260 B.C. the Roman Senate decreed that a Navy was to be built in order to make war on Carthage. A Carthaginian warship had been wrecked on the Italian coast, and the Romans were able to use this as a model and build more than a hundred ships. In the stone relief (19) a shipwright is seen at work. The Roman Navy continued to play an important part in strategy, but little or no development took place in ship design. As far as Roman soldiers were concerned, warships enabled land fighting to be carried out on water. Defensive superstructures were built on the decks, and the beaks were developed in order to do the utmost damage to the enemy ships (20). The most dangerous were those just below the surface of the water. Once Rome's empire completely encircled the Mediterranean and the Mediterranean became *mare nostra* ("our sea"), control of the seas was much easier.

19

20

21

22

Rome depended enormously on imported goods and raw materials, and, in particular, on grain from Egypt. In (23) barrels of wine are being transported in a galley ship. This impression of Rome's port of Ostia (21) shows that, although tackle had become more sophisticated and additional sails introduced, the rudder was still as primitive as ever. The ship can be seen to better advantage in a fresco in the Vatican Library (22), which shows goods being brought on board. A steering oar was needed on each side of sea-going ships because if there was any wind on the beam, the rudder oar on the windward side might rise out of the water, and be of little use. The Romans were never really a seafaring race, however, and it was left to others to develop the art of seamanship. This Danish stone relief (24) shows that medieval ships were to develop little by comparison.

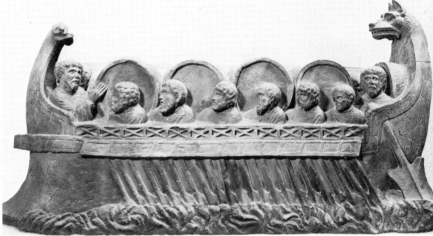

23

24

CHAPTER TWO

THE MEDIEVAL WORLD

IN THE YEAR 410, Alaric, King of the Goths, invaded the ancient city of Rome and gave it to his troops to sack. News of the event shook the civilized world. Rome had not been captured by invaders for eight hundred years. But the truth of the matter was that Rome was no longer the administrative capital of the empire. Ravenna, on the east coast of Italy, was the seat of government in the West. In fact, Rome recovered, and it was realized that Alaric's men had not caused as much destruction to the empire as they might have. But Rome was the most famous city in the world. As a symbol of the established order, its capture and sack showed that the days of the Roman Empire in the West were fast drawing to their close.

Many people, particularly pagans, thought that the fall of Rome was the direct consequence of the abolition of heathen worship, and it was in response to this claim that St. Augustine of Hippo embarked upon his monumental work, *The City of God*. The writing of its twenty-two books occupied him from 413 to 436. Even if the city of Rome should collapse in ruins, Augustine wrote, the heavenly City of God would last for ever. The Roman Empire survived in the East, based on Constantinople, but in the West the Church was the only element of stability left, in the period traditionally called the Dark Ages.

Barbarian invasions from the north and east were more than the fast disintegrating empire could cope with. In addition, Europe faced a new threat—this time from the southeast—the swelling tide of Islam. The life and teaching of Mohammed occurred at a time when the Roman Empire in the West had ceased to be a reality, and the empire in the East was exhausted by its exertions against Persia. Islam welded the various Arab tribes into a political unity strong enough to undertake the conquest of the whole of the eastern and southern empire from the Tigris to the Atlantic. This was, in fact, achieved by 700. In 711 the Moslems crossed over into Spain, and by 717 they had reached the Pyrenees. At the same time an attack was launched on Constantinople in the East, but it was able to hold out. Islam now fell into three main divisions and, after 750, seemed to settle down, alongside Christendom, for a long period of comparative calm.

What were the effects of these great events on maritime development? The Arabs took to seafaring in the Mediterranean much more quickly and easily than did the first barbarian invaders of the Roman Empire. The barbarians seemed to need the impetus of the Viking invasions before taking up commerce and seafaring on any scale. The western Mediterranean in 650 has been described as a silent lake. Only the Greeks at the eastern end carried on any maritime activity. But by 800, considerable traffic had grown between the various Islamic possessions. Cotton and cloth from Egypt, silk from the Orient, and gold and ivory from Africa were shipped to Spain; figs, wine, oil, copper, and iron went back in return. Trade was carried on with the Christian world as well, particularly with the cities of Constantinople, Amalfi, Pisa, and Narbonne. Hand in hand with commercial prosperity went culture and learning. The works of Avicenna of Baghdad were translated into Latin by Spanish Jews, and were still used as textbooks in some northern universities in 1650. Averroes of Cordova wrote commentaries on Aristotle which were introduced into France, also by Jews, and reawakened the West to Greek logical thought, and in so doing laid the foundations for modern scientific development.

From the Arabs, around 600, came a new interest in astronomy, and cosmography (world geography). The related science of navigation was therefore developed further. The Koran says: "He it is who hath appointed for you the stars that ye guide yourselves thereby in the darknesses of land and sea: we have made the signs distinct for a people who have knowledge." By the thirteenth century, so we learn from John of Monte Corvino, Arab sailors were using a rudder: "And they have a frail and flimsy rudder, like the top of a table, of a cubit in width, in the middle of the stern." The earliest European picture of a stern rudder dates from 1242, on the seal of Elbing in Germany. As a testimony to Arab skill, the court astronomers of Peking were Moslems until the Jesuits ousted them when they put the calendar in order in 1611.

A similar period of prosperity occurred in the Christian world, too, and the foundations of Venice's long supremacy in the northeastern Mediterranean were laid at this time. More than anything else, the great Crusades encouraged seagoing transport and trade. Whatever the failure of the Crusades in freeing the Holy Land, their benefit to economic life of the time was immense. Men journeyed more. The *Voyages* of Sir John Mandeville, whether compiled by him or not, are symptomatic of a desire, even a tradition, to know more, to see more, to widen one's horizons. Mandeville may never have left his fireside. Others like Marco Polo certainly did. But man was still a prisoner of the medieval world. One feels that Arab learning had little effect on medieval cosmography, for example, because it was so much part and parcel of medieval man's concept of the universe, and that concept was inextricably bound up with his religion. The time had not yet come for him to take that great series of steps forward, steps which were to catapult him into realms never before dreamed of.

Medieval European ships changed little from their predecessors over the centuries. Figure (25) shows a merchant ship from a Roman lamp, and (27) a relief from a tomb at Pompeii. The wicker-work superstructure in the twelfth-century representation of ship-building (30) is in direct line with a tradition that goes back to Homer and the ancient Greeks (compare with 9, 10). The sail was still the same shape (26), though possibly the tackle was a little more sophisticated than this illustration from an illuminated manuscript would suggest. Steering techniques had hardly improved at all (28), and for ships without a large number of oarsmen (29), there was little that could be done when the wind fell. The main new feature of medieval shipping was the greater use of sail power, necessary for voyaging in ocean and tidal waters. Another major innovation was the magnetic compass,

25

26

27

which was certainly in use at the end of the thirteenth century. In fact, the earliest-known reference occurs in the works of the monk, Alexander Neckam (1157–1217), from St. Albans in England. In his book *De utensilibus* he describes a needle used on board. This needle is put on a pivot and left to come to rest of its own accord, thus showing where the Polar star is. One ingenious early form of compass consisted of a magnetized needle inside a straw floating in a bowl of water. In *De naturis rerum*, Neckam writes: "When mariners at sea lose the quarter of the world to which they are sailing, they touch a needle with the magnet; the needle will turn round till its point will be directed towards the north." The Arabs had a form of compass, and it was probably brought by them from the Far East to the Mediterranean at the time of the Crusades.

28 29

30

During the ninth and tenth centuries the Vikings (31) sailed from Scandinavia eastward to the White Sea and westward via Iceland and Greenland to the coast of North America if the famous Vinland Map (33) is genuine. They sailed in fleets of ships between 70 and 120 feet long, propelled by oars and sails. With their high prows (36) these were strong enough to brave the open ocean and yet narrow enough to pass easily up rivers, as well as up the fjords and inlets and among the many islands of their native lands. The Vikings were fearless navigators and did not limit themselves to coastal voyages but struck out across the open sea. They would land without warning and attack and destroy—at least in their early raids. England was first attacked in 787, and the Atlantic coast of France about the same time. In 860, they entered the Mediterranean, reaching as far as Pisa in

31

33

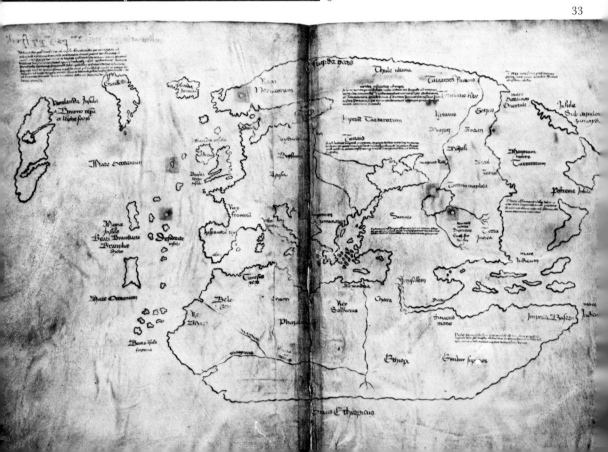

Italy. By this time, however, they had begun to settle the lands they overran. In France they founded a dukedom with Rouen as its capital. Normandy, as the dukedom was called, remained independent for almost three hundred years. Eventually a Norman Kingdom was set up in Sicily, and a band of Vikings —the Varangian Guard—worked in the service of the emperors of Constantinople.

It was from Normandy that the last real invasion of England was launched in 1066, as depicted in the seventy-two scenes of the Bayeux Tapestry. In (34) and (35) we see Harold being driven to the French coast, where he fell into the hands of William. The ships still have no rudder as such, but note the anchor, which has altered little since then, and the rowlocks for the oars. In (32) we see William's ships being built for the invasion, and in (37) the crossing of the English Channel.

24 The introduction of the compass needle was a great step forward in Western seamanship, yet the Chinese had known of it long before. It seems likely that in the late eleventh century, the Chinese already knew that the needle did not point to the true north. Yet not until the fifteenth century was the fact realized in the West. Europe owed many things to the East, despite the fact that contact between the two had been only intermittent. Domination of

Eastern routes by the Turks had made it unsafe for Westerners to voyage eastward. Also the situation in the West was far too unsettled for most Europeans to think of leaving home. However, the conquests of Genghis Khan and the reign of his grandson, Kublai Khan, enabled the author of an Italian handbook of about 1340 to write: "The road you travel from Tana [on the Black Sea] to Cathay [China] is perfectly safe, whether by

day or by night, according to what the merchants say who have used it." Although trade flourished in these conditions, depicted in this early woodcut (39), men like Sir John Mandeville were interested in travel for its own sake. He is pictured here (38, 40) in two scenes from his travels; but it is doubtful how much he actually saw of what he described. It was these conditions which aided the journeys of the Venetian Marco Polo who, at the end of the thirteenth century, crossed Asia and in all spent seventeen years in China. His account of his travels inspired artists to illustrate the marvels he described, though it was not until some fifty years after his death that the information he supplied was incorporated into maps like this one (42) showing the Persian Gulf and Caspian Sea. We also see his departure from Venice (41) and some of the strange countryside through which he passed (43).

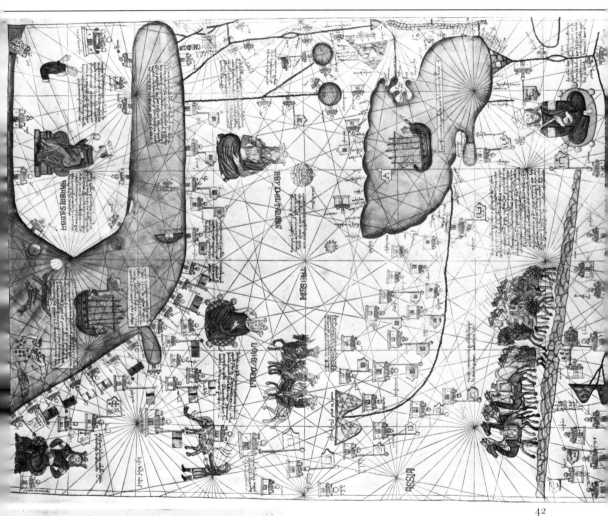

42

43

CHAPTER THREE

INDIA AND THE INDIES

FIFTEENTH-CENTURY EUROPE was much more concerned with survival in the face of the Ottoman Turks, who were then sweeping all before them, than with overseas expansion. There had indeed been an earlier period of European expansion, as we have seen in the previous chapter. Marco Polo had reached the court of Kublai Khan, and the Norsemen had reached Greenland and even perhaps America. But all that was long ago. It was true that commerce between the cities of northern Italy and Asia had continued and developed via Baghdad and Constantinople, and helped increase European knowledge of the world. But the new Turkish threat on both land and sea suddenly threw the whole future of these links into jeopardy. Constantinople itself fell in 1453. Yet although it looked to some people as if this was the beginning of the end for Europe, it was in fact the start of a new and brighter phase. The sudden arrival of leading *émigré* Byzantine scholars in the West, with their valuable manuscripts and Greek traditions gave great stimulus at the time. The process of rediscovering ancient learning (including mathematics) had already been going on for well over a century. But the fall of Constantinople signified that from that moment the initiative for survival and renewal had to be firmly grasped by the West. In this sense, it can rightly be regarded as a milestone in Western history.

In the meantime Europe could not live on scholarship alone. With the Turkish threat to her commerce, eyes were turned elsewhere. Of all the nations most likely to embark on voyages of discovery at this time, it was the Portuguese who first began to think about the possibilities of the Atlantic Ocean. Might it lead ultimately to trade with the East, rather than simply enclose the western horizon of Europe? Portugal was particularly well placed because the Moors had been driven out of their country comparatively early on. As a result, Portugal had found stability and peace at a time when other nations lacked it. England and France were both plunged in wars at home and abroad, and the Spaniards were occupied in chasing out the Moors from the peninsula or fighting among themselves. There was the broadening influence of the Renaissance at work, also. The population of Portugal began to increase, but the homeland was too poor and too small to support any sizeable increase. Portugal needed some kind of expansion. There was also her geographical location to be considered. If a westward route lay across the Atlantic to the mystic East, then Portugal was well situated to exploit it.

Ever since Marco Polo had written of his travels in China, men's minds had been turned toward this ancient land. Marco Polo himself came from Venice, itself probably as rich and cultured a city as any at the time. How much more exotic, then, must his description of Hangchow have seemed to the people of a small medieval town in Europe. "I will tell you all its nobleness," he wrote, "for without doubt it is the largest city in the world. . . . The merchants are so numerous and so rich that their wealth can neither be told nor believed. On each of the . . . bridges ten men keep guard by day and night, so that no one may dare to raise a disturbance, or commit theft or homicide. . . . All the streets are paved with stones and bricks; and so are the high roads of Manji [South China]."

Meanwhile, marked developments in the art of seafaring had been taking place in fifteenth-century Europe. The magnetic variation of the compass was now known, so that navigation was set to become a more accurate science. But most compasses were still rather primitive. As William Barlowe wrote in his *Magnetical Advertisement* of 1616: "The Compass Needle, being the most admirable and useful instrument of the whole world, is both amongst ours and other nations, for the most part, so bungerly and absurdly contrived, as nothing more." But there had been immense advances in the design and manufacture of masts and sails. As G. S. L. Clowes writes in his *Sailing Ships*: "In 1400 northern ships were entirely dependent on a fair wind, and were quite unable—and never attempted—to make headway against an adverse wind, while before 1500 ships had been able to make the long ocean voyages which had resulted

in Columbus' discovery of America, Diaz's doubling of the Cape of Good Hope, and the opening of the Indian trade route by Vasco da Gama."

As we shall now see, one man more than anyone else—Prince Henry the Navigator —was responsible for the Portuguese advance in the realms of seafaring. Prince Henry's expeditions discovered, or rediscovered, the islands off western Africa —Madeira, the Azores, and Cape Verde. These islands provided useful bases for yet more extensive voyages. Henry died before his work was finished, but King John II took up his interest and organized a system whereby the African trade was licensed by the Portuguese government to merchants. In return, the merchants had to explore and chart another 100 miles of the coastline each year. Thanks to their efforts, and eventually those of Diaz and Da Gama, the King of Portugal was proudly able to style himself "Lord of the Conquest, Navigation, and Commerce of Ethiopia, Persia and India."

Unfortunately for the Portuguese, they were unable to keep hold of their empire for long, and finally the Dutch and English moved in behind them. By and large, the Dutch took the islands and the English the mainland. Although the Portuguese were generally able administrators, they treated the native populations no more sympathetically than the Dutch, for example, and their departure was not always a matter of regret for the natives.

Prince Henry the Navigator, 1394–1460 (44), laid the foundations of Portugal's maritime greatness at the naval centre of Sagres. Under his inspiration, Portuguese ships pressed farther and farther down the Atlantic coast of Africa in an attempt to find a new way to the East. In 1487 Bartholemeu Diaz rounded the Cape of Good Hope and turned northward into the Indian Ocean. The alarmed crew insisted on returning, however, and it was left to Vasco da Gama ten years later, to complete what Diaz had begun (45).

Once the way to India lay open, the Portuguese were obliged to assert their presence in the Indian Ocean because they were, in fact, challenging what had until then been the undisputed trading rights of the Arabs. Nevertheless, the West was able to learn much from

44

45

46

the Arab world. Arab sailors were at this time more skilled navigators, as their maps and instruments show. Figure 46 shows an engraved bronze dial very similar to that made for Sir Francis Drake (280).

From fifteenth-century Lisbon (47) administrators like the great Albuquerque (48) were sent out to gain control of trade on the Malabar coast. After fortifying Goa, he seized Malacca and sent a small fleet to the Moluccas. The Spice Islands had been rounded at last. Local natives provided manpower for the ships like these of Malabar (49), though by and large Albuquerque did not exploit them. The Portuguese success excited the anger and envy of other powers, such as Venice, where prayers were actually said in church for the success of the Arabs.

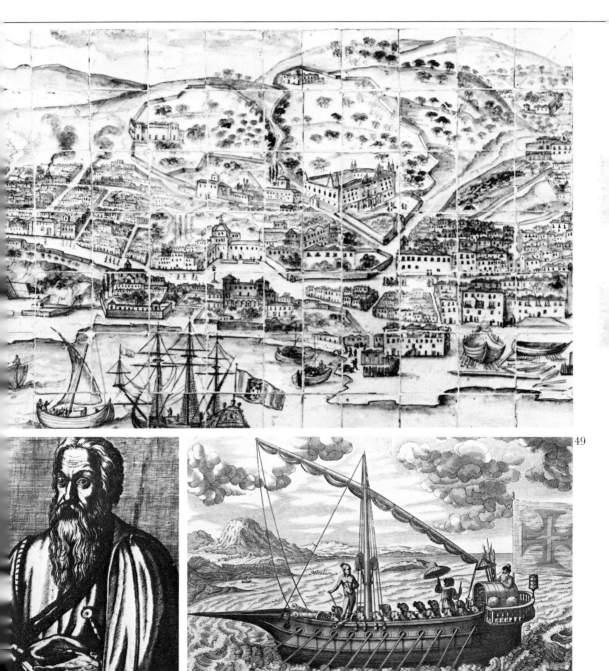

49

The oar-driven galley of the Mediterranean was replaced by the caravel, an example of which is given here (50). The caravel was similar to the ships built for the Navy of Henry VIII of England. The *Unicorn* was a fairly typical vessel; this illustration is taken from an inventory of the time (51). Ships like the *Golden Hind*, in which Sir Francis Drake (55) circumnavigated the world, also resemble the caravel. This picture of the *Golden Hind* (52) is taken from Hondius' map of Drake's voyages, first published around the year 1580. The caravels greatly facilitated the Portuguese advance on the seas. They could put out to the open sea, were easily handled, and could ride out storms with much less harm to themselves than the great galleons. In the sixteenth century, Portuguese sailors seemed to be

50

51

52

literally everywhere, and Camoëns, their greatest poet, wrote with pride: "Had there been more of the world they would have discovered it."

As Portuguese viceroy in India, Albuquerque set up his capital at Goa (53). He was a wise and successful administrator, and was three times confirmed in his office. However, he became such a powerful figure in his own right, that King Emmanuel decided to remove him in 1515, after eight years of rule. Later he relented, only to learn that Albuquerque had since died. Later, in 1523, Vasco da Gama was made viceroy, but by this time he was already over sixty, and tired. His rule lasted for just over a year. An early manuscript portrait of him is reproduced here (54). He died at Cochin on Christmas Day in 1524.

Man & Woman of Goa.

53

54

55

Dom Vasco da gama

The Italian, Toscanelli, had already begun to wonder whether it might be possible to reach "India" by sailing westward across the Atlantic. (Columbus took some pains to conceal his debt to Toscanelli later in life.) However, no one suspected that such a great continent—America—lay in this direction. All memory of the early Viking voyages had long been forgotten; the old Viking colony on Greenland died out by about the year 1450. It was Magellan, a Portuguese in the service of Spain, who first realized that America lay between Europe and the Spice Islands, and consequently set out to find a way around the land mass (56, upper left). In 1520, his tiny ship, *Victoria*, picked its way through the straits that now bear Magellan's name (56, centre left) and so into the Pacific Ocean. Unfortunately, Magellan was killed while taking

56
57

part in a local war in the Philippines, but his second-in-command, Juan Sebastián del Cano (56, upper right), took the ship on around the Cape of Good Hope and brought the expedition home. It was then quite clear that America and the Indies were different places. In 1577 Sir Francis Drake also sailed around the world (56, lower left) in his *Golden Hind* (57). The cup shown here (58) is engraved with a map of the world in memory of the voyage. He was blown off course and discovered that there was open sea south of what became known as Cape Horn, but, in fact he went on through the straits as Magellan had done. It was left to the Dutchman, Willem Cornelis Schouten, to round Cape Horn in 1616 (59) and name it after his birthplace, Hoorn in Holland. He is seen landing on Horn Island (60), and in (61) the Dutch are seen at Port Desire hunting sea lion for food.

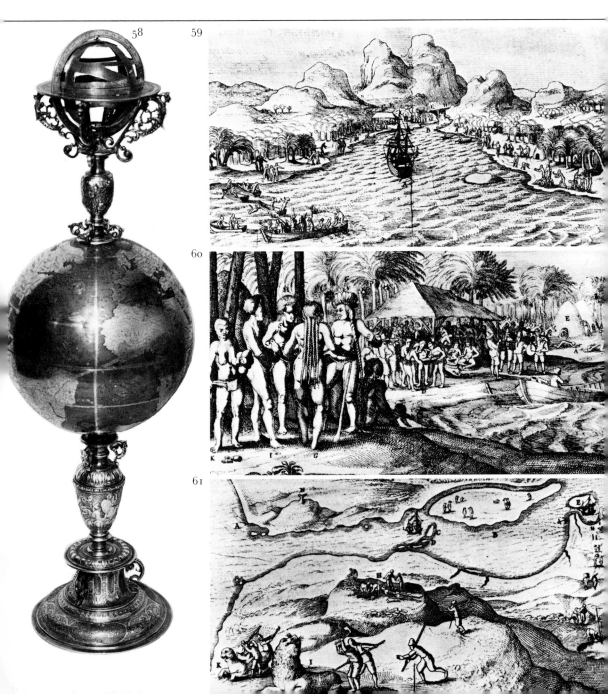

34 The Portuguese empire, beating off Turkish attacks, flourished for a century. But the strain on the manpower resources of such a small nation began to take its toll. Toward the end of the sixteenth century Portugal became involved in fighting in Morocco, and was then annexed by Philip II of Spain. The effort to retain her empire was too great, and the Moluccas, or Spice Islands, to which much of her exploratory energies had been directed, fell to the Dutch in 1613. Natives of these islands are pictured in this rare engraving (62). Timor, an East Indian Island, was divided between the Portuguese and the Dutch, and the Dutch East India Company was set up. The English East India Company had been set up in 1600, to stake English claims to the East. Figure (64) depicts some Timorian natives. Eventually Java, where the Portuguese had founded trading factories, fell to the Dutch

62 63
64

also. Figure (63) shows a merchant of Java.

A Portuguese ship arrived in China at Canton in 1516, and on the pattern of developments elsewhere in the Far East, the Dutch and English followed, in fact, by the end of the century. Figures (65, 67) are pictures of Emperors of China drawn by early Western voyagers. A similar sequence of events took place in Japan, although there the authorities actively encouraged the English and Dutch at the expense of the Portuguese. Figure (66) shows Japanese praying for the souls of their parents during a religious ceremony. For a century the Japanese welcomed strangers and trade; Christian missionaries and converts followed, though for a time only the Dutch were allowed to remain. However, both China and Japan eventually expelled the foreigners, and Japan remained closed to the West until the visit of Commodore Perry in 1853.

65 66
67

CHAPTER FOUR

AMERICA AND CIRCUMNAVIGATION

IN THEIR EAGERNESS to find a new route to the East, navigators never suspected the existence of a continent between Europe and China and Japan. Since the Portuguese had opened up the route to India, and the Venetians were too busy in the Mediterranean, the Genoese were free to explore the new possibilities. Genoa's power was declining at this time, however. When she lost the last of her possessions in the Crimea in 1475, it seemed that the city of Genoa might sink into oblivion. But the Genoese themselves ensured that the fame of their birthplace would survive. They were everywhere in Europe, particularly as shipbuilders, and many were already in the service of Spain and Portugal.

The Italian, Toscanelli, had put forward the idea that it was possible to reach India by sailing westward across the Atlantic. Christopher Columbus, himself a Genoese sailor, set to work to prove this theory. Columbus was convinced that Japan lay only a few days' voyage from Lisbon. Since the Portuguese would not sponsor him, he had to turn to the Spaniards for help. He proposed a voyage for gold and spices, and a mission for the conversion of the heathens of Asia. In this way he induced Queen Isabella of Castile to provide three ships for him. Even so, in the eyes of many people, his ideas about "discovery" were a wrong and wasteful use of energy which should have been better employed in more weighty matters.

Spain itself was still trying to drive out the Moors; and there was also the Turkish menace to the whole of Europe. In the face of the growing power of the Turkish Empire, there seemed little point in setting out to explore barren wastes across the ocean when the existence of Europe itself seemed to be threatened. Such was the concern with the menace from the East that, for example, twice as many books were published in sixteenth-century France about Turkey than about America. Even when new and distant colonies began to produce revenue for Spain and Portugal, the home governments remained very inward-looking, and hardly concerned themselves with what went on abroad.

Furthermore, when the colonies began to ship their produce home, the sudden vast influx of gold in Spain had an extremely unsettling effect on the economy. As Sir Walter Raleigh said: "It is this Indian gold that endangereth and disturbeth all the nations of Europe." Raleigh himself was one of the most indefatigable searchers for the fabled gold of El Dorado. The discovery of America, or "the Indies," was not entirely welcomed by Europe. The impact of Asia and Africa on Europe was, in some ways, more important than that of America. As Professor Hugh Trevor-Roper has written: "In Africa the Portuguese discovery of Ethiopia revealed an ancient Christian Kingdom which had never been subject to the Pope. That excited the Reformers in Europe. In Asia the Chinese Empire revealed a government which would long be an ideal for Europe. The three continents were interdependent too. American bullion was used to buy Asiatic spices, and African slave labour was needed to work the American sugar plantations. All three continents together built up a new dimension of European experience."

Few people thought of it in those terms at that time. The Portuguese concentrated on their Eastern route, and the Spaniards on the West. Both did their best to keep their routes secret. In such circumstances they can hardly have expected to find interdependence at work. In the broadest terms, however, the prevalent atmosphere was one of expansion, discovery, and a general feeling of change—not always for the best, as some people thought.

Gradually, the increase in circulation of money minted from New World bullion made people realize the need for a balance of trade. Thomas Mun (1571–1641) wrote: "The ordinary means to increase our wealth and treasure is by foreign trade wherein we must ever observe this rule; to sell more to strangers yearly than we consume of theirs in value, because that part of our stock which is not returned to us in wares must necessarily be brought home in treasure." It is not quite as simple as that, but he was clearly thinking on the right lines. In any case, balance of trade figures present problems of accurate estimating even in a system as statistically

oriented as our own at the present time. It was even more difficult in an age when statistics were anyone's guess. The value of money, too, fluctuated wildly, and rulers could ignore their creditors, as did Philip II of Spain when he broke the Fuggers' Bank. A secondary result of this action was to remove the centre of European finance from Augsburg (and, to a lesser extent, Hamburg) to Amsterdam, almost in anticipation of the future expansion of the Dutch interests overseas.

Trade, then, was the great incentive in the age of the explorers. But when it came to colonization, the picture was somewhat different. Some colonies, certainly, were founded on a speculative basis, and Dutch colonization was closely allied to commercial considerations. France, in refusing to allow Huguenots to settle in Canada, deprived it of the very people who could have given it prosperity. In the last analysis, it was religious considerations that made colonization a success in North America, since the first effective and continuous settlement (though not actually the first in time) was that of the Pilgrim Fathers in 1620.

Modern scholars tend to play down the importance of the actual *Mayflower* voyage, but as a symbol of the spirit that made North America, no one can diminish its significance. Those pilgrims did not go in the expectation of profit but because they wanted to live in the way they chose. In the New World they found this freedom.

The earliest surviving printed map to show the discovery of the New World is the Contarini map in the British Museum, London, dating from 1506. The Ruysch map of 1508 (68) was drawn on a projection very similar to that of Contarini, but had more up-to-date information on it. Greenland ("Gruenlant") appears at the top, and the Caribbean coastline of South America at the bottom, just above the line of the Equator. But possibly the most famous of the early maps is that by Martin Waldseemüller, dating from 1507. In the portion of it shown here (71), Amerigo Vespucci is depicted, and in fact this was the first map to use the name "America" to designate the New World. It was ironical that, despite the fact that it was Columbus who discovered America, the name of another person should have been given to it. Vespucci claimed to have made four voyages to America,

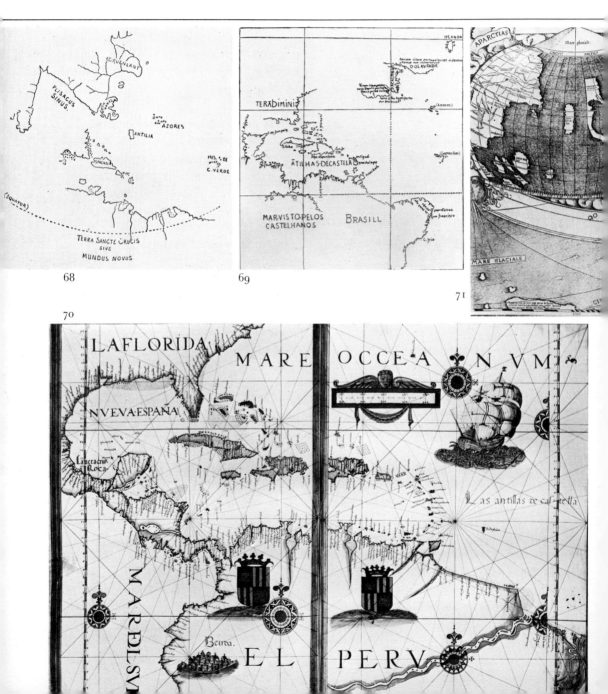

68

69

71

70

but he did not, in fact, command any of them. An educated man from Florence, he first worked as a commercial agent. His family was of some standing in Florence, and he became chief pilot of the school of navigation in Seville.

Gradually the maps of the New World became more detailed. Here is a Portuguese chart dating from 1520 (69) showing rather more knowledge of the Caribbean and the mid-continental coastline. Another Portuguese chart dates from 1565 (70). The number of place names is itself a testimony to the discoveries which had been made by this time. This English map (72) produced in the reign of Henry VIII inspires less confidence. The coastlines on the French map by Pierre Desceliers are more accurate (73), although some of the detail suggested by its illustrations is highly imaginative. Maps of the time, like books, were often beautifully decorated.

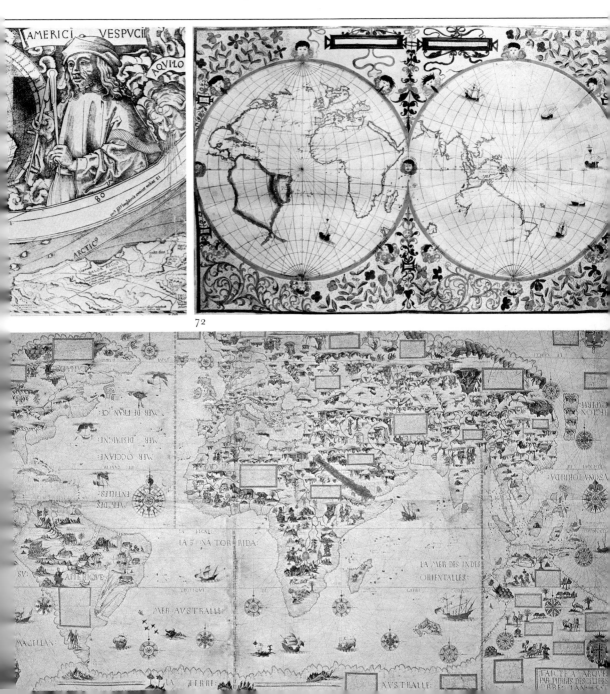

72

40 Here is a portrait of Christopher Columbus, engraved from the painting by Lotto (74). Columbus set sail in the *Santa Maria* from Palos in August, 1492; this woodcut (75) impression of his ship is said to have been made from a sketch of Columbus himself, and was first published in 1494. Thirty-three days after leaving Palos, Columbus sighted the outer Cays of the Bahamas. In this woodcut, the Atlantic Ocean is represented as little more than a river (77). Whatever the original object of his expedition, Columbus thought that San Salvador (76, middle right) was an outlying island of Asia. This sketch map is sometimes attributed to Columbus. On his return to Europe, Columbus was obliged to put in for shelter in the River Tagus. The Portuguese authorities were anxious to know what he had been doing, and decided to lay claim to his discoveries. Following the pro-

clamation of two Papal bulls, the Treaty of Tordesillas was signed between Spain and Portugal in 1494. Under the treaty the newly discovered lands were divided into Spanish and Portuguese spheres of influence. In fact, the treaty put part of South America (including much of what is today Brazil) into the lap of Portugal. Before the treaty was signed, however, Columbus sailed back to the West Indies in an attempt to settle the island of Hispaniola. On his first voyage to Hispaniola, Columbus had obtained gold by bartering with the natives, as shown in the illustration here (78). Then, in 1499, the Margarita pearl fishery was discovered on the Venezuelan coast, and it was soon developed as a profitable concern. Unfortunately, this development entailed a cruel use of slaves as pearl divers (79); such cruelty was to dog the conquest of the New World.

79

42 While Columbus was consolidating his discoveries, Henry VII of England granted permission to John Cabot, a Bristol man of Venetian origin, to sail across the north Atlantic in search of new lands. There was already a good deal of traffic between Lisbon, Bristol, Ireland, and Iceland, and there were tales of lands farther west. So it was that Cabot became the first man to sail the Atlantic by the northern route after the Vikings (apart from the old Greenlanders until about 1450). Already in 1500 his discovery was shown on the map (81) produced by Juan de la Cosa, who sailed with Columbus on his second voyage. Cabot's son, Sebastian (83), was to carry on his father's tradition of seamanship. The Portuguese map (80) of John and Sebastian Cabot's discoveries dates from 1544.

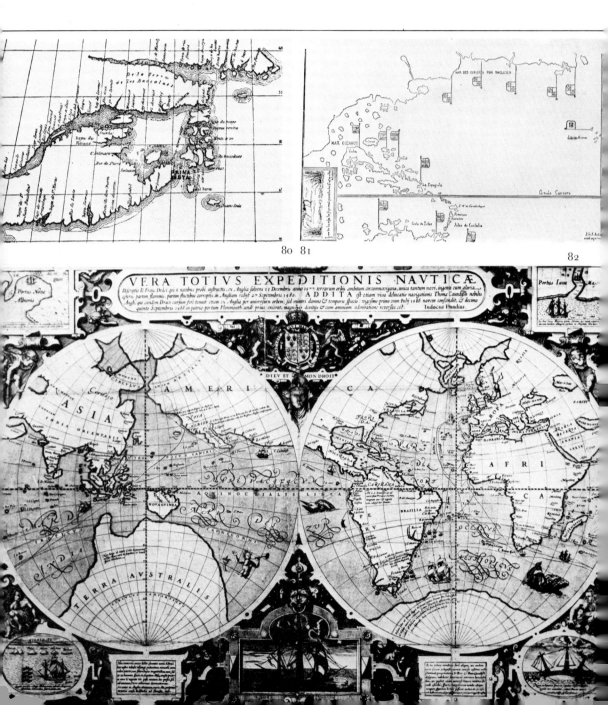

80 81

82

VERA TOTIVS EXPEDITIONIS NAVTICÆ

But Sebastian Cabot did not confine himself to one particular field of exploration. He also sailed to South America, and the fact that he succeeded Amerigo Vespucci as chief pilot of the school of navigation in Seville put him in company with those, like Magellan and Drake, whose vision was truly global. Magellan's ship, *Victoria*, is depicted here (84). The Hondius map (82) commemorates Drake's voyages around the world, shown by an unbroken line. The dotted line represents Thomas Cavendish's voyage of 1586–8. By 1633 Hondius also republished Gerhard Mercator's detailed map of South America (85), though here Tierra del Fuego is shown as a part of a southern land mass, despite the fact that Schouten had sailed around Cape Horn in 1616.

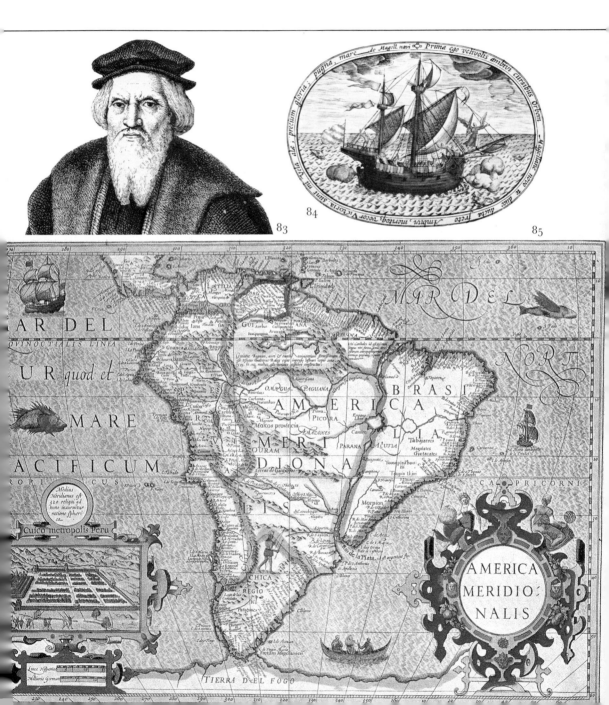

83

84

85

In 1513, Vasco de Balboa, a Spanish adventurer, crossed the Isthmus of Darien and became the first European to see the Pacific. Balboa and people like him did not endure the hardships they encountered because they were looking for a western route to China and India. They were looking for gold, and they were prepared to stop at nothing to find it. This early woodcut (86) shows Indians bringing treasure to Balboa, and (88) gold dust. In the face of such an attitude, the natives frequently killed both themselves and their children rather than endure the brutalities inflicted on them by the newcomers (87). Balboa was the first of the *conquistadores*, as they were known, and he was followed by many such men.

Francisco Pizarro, one of five brothers, set out from Darien also, but in 1530, for the con-

86

87

88

quest of Peru. Here (89) he is seen journeying with a team of native bearers. Cuzco, the Inca capital, was taken in November, 1533. Figure (90) depicts Peruvian people from an early engraving. But Pizarro decided to found a new capital, which he called Lima, near the sea. The silver extracted from Peru became very important to Spain. Events were later to show, however, that the choice of Lima was a very shortsighted one. It merely emphasized the difference between the coast, which was predominantly Spanish, and the largely Indian-dominated mountains. The Spanish central government eventually decided to send in its own men, and one by one all the brothers were removed. Francisco was assassinated in 1541 and Gonzalo beheaded at Cuzco in 1548 (91).

89

90

91

46   In 1519, the year that Balboa was beheaded for treason, Hernando Cortes (93) began his famous expedition against the Aztecs. Purely by chance the Aztecs were expecting the return of their god Quetzalcoatl at the same time as Cortes arrived, and embassies were sent to him from the leader Montezuma with gifts, threats, and pleas of poverty in an attempt to dissuade the Spaniards from attacking the capital, Tenochtitlán. The pleas of poverty did not convince the Spaniards when they saw the richness of the gifts. It was at this point that Cortes' psychological insight came into operation. He saw into the Aztec character and determined to increase his own reputation while playing on the Aztecs' fears. His meeting with their leader, Montezuma, has inspired artists and playwrights from that day to the present. This representation (92) is by an Aztec, who also recorded the arrival of

92

93

Spaniards in the New World (94). The Spaniards were welcomed as guests into the Aztec capital, which Cortes eventually took and destroyed, razing it to the ground and building a completely Spanish city on the site.

The inhospitable region of Patagonia, at the southern tip of South America, did not excite the interest of the *conquistadores*. For the most part it was a barren and inaccessible territory. But it did lie on the southern route to the Pacific, and as such was known to many sailors, if not particularly well. On his voyage of circumnavigation, Drake had to suppress a mutiny at St. Julian's Bay (95) by beheading the leader. Notions about the size of the Patagonians seem to have remained vague until the eighteenth century at least (96). But a new school of explorers was arriving in the New World, to whom we owe a great deal including the Frenchman Father Louis Hennepin (97).

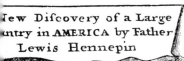

New Discovery of a Large Country in AMERICA by Father Lewis Hennepin

95 96
97

A Sailor giving a Patagonian Woman some Biscuit for her Child?

Gent. Mag. May. 1767

In 1535, Jacques Cartier explored the Bay of Fundy and the St. Lawrence River (98). In fact, Cartier, like Henry Hudson in the *Half Moon* after him (99), was looking for a north-west passage around America. Not until his third voyage, however, was any attempt at colonization made, and unfortunately this proved to be a failure. It was the beginning of the next century before another attempt was made, this time in Acadia, or Nova Scotia as it became known. Then, in 1608, Samuel de Champlain founded the settlement of Quebec (100). De Champlain wanted to develop Quebec as a fort and centre for trade, rather than as a colony in the wider sense. As one might expect, French colonization was a much more widely planned affair than that of either the English or the Spanish. There was much more organization of settlement, and each colony was ruled by a military governor

98

99

100

appointed by the crown. Financial and economic matters, however, were handled by an Intendant, who acted as both an adviser and as a check on the military. All organization was centralized under officials in Paris. Furthermore, the French did not wish the colonies to become havens for all the rejects of society, as did the English to a large extent (although, of course, the Puritans were a strong element in both cases). Under Jean-

Baptiste Colbert, the population of French Canada trebled, and by 1673 Jesuit missionaries had explored most of the land around the Great Lakes. One of them, Hennepin, has left posterity some delightful drawings of what he saw (101, 102). In 1682 Robert de la Salle made a journey down the whole length of the Mississippi to the Gulf of Mexico, but in 1684, while trying to found Louisiana (103), he lost his life.

101

102

103

Queen Elizabeth I of England (104) was much more interested in sharing in the gains of attacks on foreign vessels than in founding colonies abroad. Finance was frequently a problem for her, and indeed, with the threat to her throne represented by Mary Queen of Scots and the Spanish Armada, for example, she had too many concerns at home to think of empire. However, Sir Humphrey Gilbert decided to make an attempt at settlement in North America, and it was under his inspiration that Newfoundland became the first English possession in the New World. At Gilbert's death the ill-starred Sir Walter Raleigh obtained a patent from the queen to found a settlement called Virginia in her honour, and an initial voyage was made in 1584. The following year the first settlers arrived, and set themselves up on Roanoke Island, off the coast of North Carolina (107).

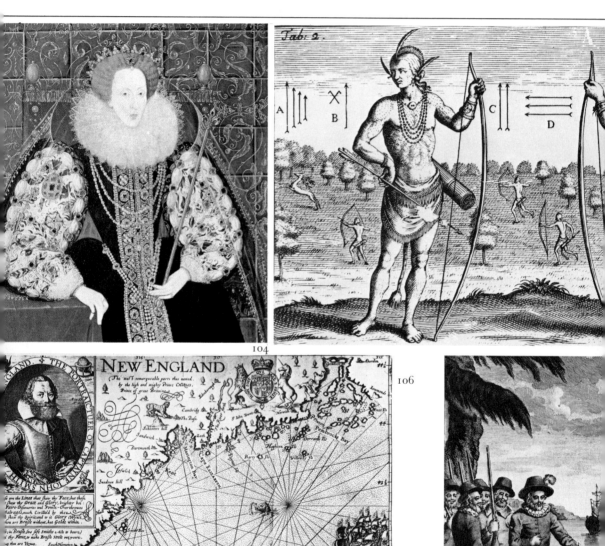

The original colony did not survive, but the seeds had in any case been sown. In 1606 the Virginia Company was formed, and although it failed in 1623, by then Virginia had found its salvation—in tobacco. It was probably due to the first governor, Captain John Smith (106), more than anyone else, that the colony managed to survive. Smith was an excellent leader, a firm disciplinarian, and he also enjoyed good relations with the Indians. Re-produced below are three woodcuts which record some Indian occupations observed by English visitors. Figure (105) gives two impressions of a warlike Indian ruler armed with bow and arrows, and wearing a primitive headdress. Figure (108) shows Indians making canoes, and felling trees. The trees are felled by fires rather than axes. Figure (109) shows the wife of an Indian chief and her child, with two pipes of peace.

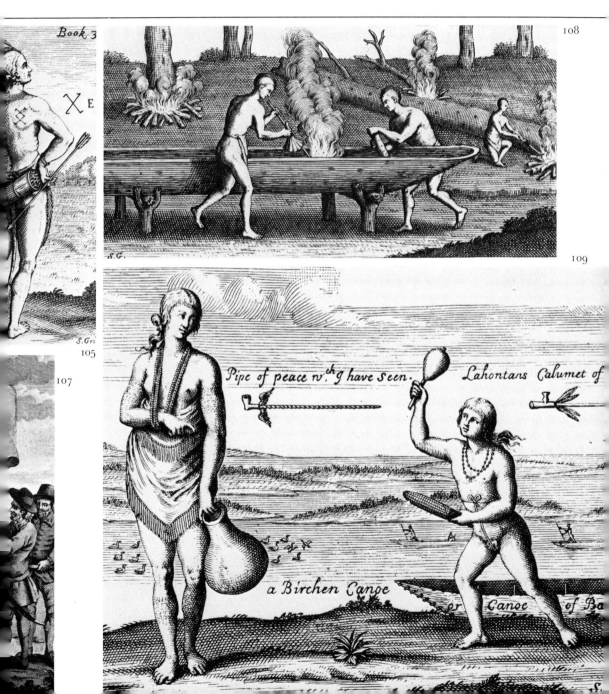

CHAPTER FIVE

AUSTRALASIA

WHEN SOME of America's offshore islands were first discovered by Christopher Columbus, the very existence of a continent of America was completely unsuspected. To the end of his life, Columbus probably never realized exactly what he had discovered. Even if the Vikings had previously reached America, no one in fifteenth-century Europe remembered it. But the existence of Australia—the subject of the next chapter—was known long before anyone set out to explore it. The reason for its neglect was a very particular one. The route to India around Africa and the expeditions westward across the Atlantic to reach the Orient were inspired by commercial enterprise. There was a strong incentive to succeed. But the Dutch had been sailing past Australia for years. They knew perfectly well that there was land there in some form. They even called it New Holland, but having decided that it had no commercial value, they left it alone. Even when Captain James Cook took up where Abel Janszoon Tasman had left off, and charted and claimed the coast of what was later called New South Wales, the best use the British government could devise for the new region was to turn it into a penal colony.

One might well ask why Cook even bothered to set out to chart these coasts. In fact, his first voyage (1768–71) was made ostensibly to observe the course of the planet Venus over the Pacific in June, 1769. Alexander Dalrymple, a geographer

of distinction, had been chosen by the Royal Society to lead the mission. George III approved the idea, arranged for the Navy to provide ships, and allocated £4,000 to the society for expenses. The Admiralty, however, refused to let Dalrymple, a non-Naval man, command one of their ships. By virtue of the work he had already done in Canada, Captain Cook was the obvious choice. His task was made somewhat easier, as we shall see, by the return of H.M.S. *Dolphin*, under Captain Samuel Wallis, three months before Cook was due to set sail. Wallis had discovered Tahiti, and this was to be Cook's destination. But when *Endeavour* finally set sail, Cook received secret instructions from the Admiralty as well as his general instructions. After the transit of Venus had taken place, he was to sail southward in an attempt to discover the Great South Land—*terra australis incognita*. In the event of not finding it, he was to head for New Zealand, which Tasman had discovered but barely explored more than a hundred years before. Dalrymple believed that New Zealand was part of the great continent. Cook's task was to explore the coast of New Zealand and then return.

A few days after his departure, the *London Gazette* announced that Cook had left "to attempt some new discoveries in that vast unknown tract above the latitude 40." So much for the secret instructions. The most important feature about the

Endeavour for future exploration was that it was the first ship to sail with a team of scientists aboard. Voyages of discovery had now entered on an entirely new and scientific phase of development.

After he had failed to find any land in latitude 40, Cook sailed on to New Zealand and realized that it consisted of two separate islands. It was then decided, at a meeting of officers, to voyage on to the coast of New Holland—the future New South Wales—and sail home around the Cape of Good Hope. Cook would have liked to have returned via Cape Horn in order to make quite certain that there was no land in that region. Unfortunately, the weather and time of year were unsuitable. Cook then explored the whole eastern coast of Australia, and went on to Batavia, Cape Town, and so to England. Of the voyage Cook himself wrote: "I have made no very great discoveries, yet I have explored more of the Great South Sea than all who have gone before me, and little remains now to be done." He had not proved beyond any shadow of doubt that there was no southern continent. But the possible area in which it could lie was, thanks to Cook, greatly reduced. The public purpose of Cook's voyage—the observation of the transit of Venus—had been a failure. But then so had all the other attempts at observation. Venus is surrounded by a thick halo which made it very difficult for the beginning and end of the transit to be recorded accurately.

Dalrymple still insisted, however, that a southern continent existed somewhere, and so a new voyage was planned for Cook—this time to circumnavigate the world in the region of the Antarctic Circle. We shall examine this aspect of his second voyage later, and since a good deal of it concerns the Pacific, that, too, is dealt with later.

One cannot ignore the contribution made by the early Dutch navigators and the Spaniard, Luis Vaez de Torres, but it was Cook who finally drew the attention of the Western world to Australasia and, in his own words, little remained to be done. Of course, the attitude of governments toward acquiring territory had changed in the interval. By the end of the eighteenth century, empire for its own sake had an appeal it hardly had before. Perhaps too much has been made of the fact that Cook was misguided in thinking that certain parts of Australia were suitable for cultivation. Yet it must be borne in mind that his main task was to chart the coast. He found it extremely difficult, and almost impossible to make contact with the natives, which would have helped him to determine the nature of the country more easily. But the whole Australian venture was, in a way, an unexpected bonus for the English government. Even when the actual existence of the continent was known, a further century elapsed before anyone crossed it in both directions, let alone adequately mapped it.

It is to the activities of the Dutch in the Far East (110) that the world owes much of its knowledge of that region, and in particular the southern part. Although the Dutch voyages were, for the most part, made purely for commercial reasons, they greatly benefited European knowledge of the Far East in general. In the sixteenth century the world maps of Mercator and Ortelius (227, 232) on pages 98 and 99, showed *terra australis* as a continuous land mass separated by straits from South America and South Africa. Gradually the efforts of generations nibbled away at the extent of this unknown region, until it was shown on subsequent maps as a mere vestige around the South Pole, or disappeared entirely.

The continent known today as Australia was discovered as a result of Dutch commerce. In 1606 Willem Jansz encountered the coasts of New Guinea and northeast Australia,

110

111

112

although he did not realize that they were separate land masses. In the same year the Spanish navigator, Luis Vaez de Torres, sailed through the straits that bear his name, between New Guinea and Australia, again without realizing it. Part of the coast of southwest Australia was discovered by two Dutchmen, Dirck Hartogszoon and Cornelis de Houtman, in 1616 and 1619 respectively. The breakthrough came in 1642, however, when Abel Tasman (112) sailed out from Batavia, around Australia, along the coast of New Guinea and back, discovering Tasmania and New Zealand on the way (111). He had an uncomfortable encounter with Maoris in Murderer's Bay (113) and a calm one with natives of the Bismarck Archipelago (114). Tasman named the island he discovered Van Dieman's Land after the then governor of the Dutch East Indies. His voyage is shown in (115).

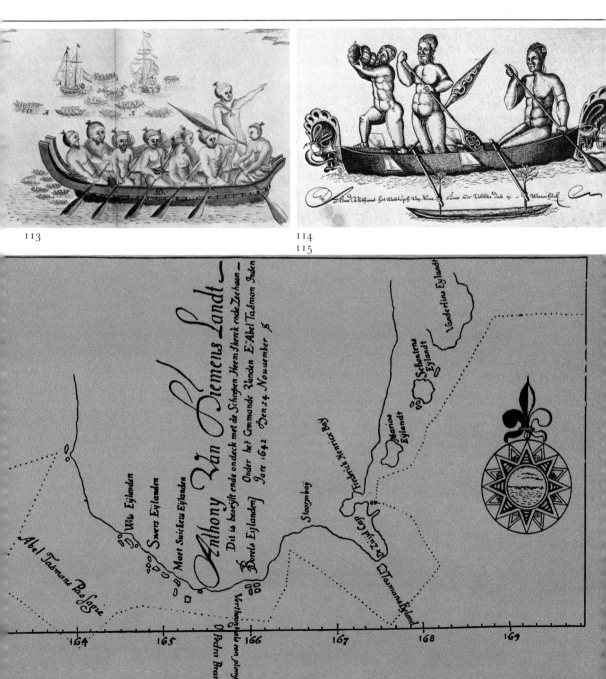

113

114
115

Although much new land had been discovered, the trading companies that employed the sailors or financed them were primarily interested in commerce; they were reluctant to invest money simply in the interests of furthering geographical knowledge. More than a century passed before any systematic exploration and charting began, and one man in particular, James Cook, led the field. It is fitting that the strait that separates North and South Island of New Zealand (116) should bear his name. Of course, there had been other explorers and navigators, such as the Frenchman Louis de Bougainville, 1729–1811 (118), but no one else measures up to the stature of Cook in this field.

In more secular and more prosaic times, the names the explorers gave to their discoveries were equally secular and prosaic. Cascade Cove in Dusky Bay (117) hardly

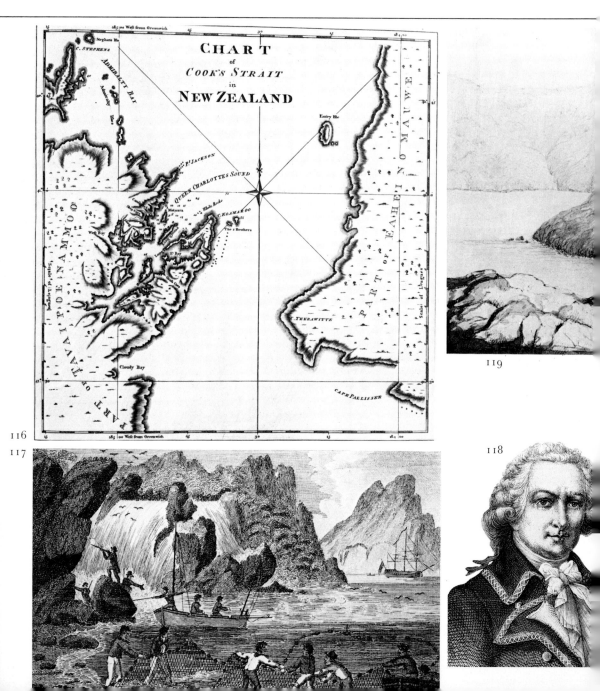

116

117

118

119

compares with the names of saints and Latinized Christian names of monarchs that the fifteenth, sixteenth, and seventeenth—and to some extent the earlier eighteenth—centuries bestowed on places. And yet, doubtless, future generations will find them almost as romantic. Certainly the appearance and culture of the natives fired the imagination of the late eighteenth-century explorers, with distinctive houses and exotic canoes with fantastically carved and ornamented prows and sterns (121). It was left to a later generation to explore the more remote regions and appreciate some of the natural beauties of the country, as in the two paintings of Thompson's Sound and Milford Sound on Middle Island, dating from 1850 and 1851 respectively (119, 120). In the days before photography had been invented, painters took great pains to leave accurate records of what they saw.

120

It was Captain James Cook (124), 1728–79, in the *Endeavour* (125)—a model of which is shown here—who charted the coast of New Zealand and New South Wales, or New Holland as it was then called (122). At one point his ship lay for twenty-three hours on the rocks at the mouth of the Endeavour River (123)—for location see bottom left-hand corner of (122)—and he had to lay the ship up for repairs. In the same year Cook had discovered Botany Bay (127), and there he formally took possession of New South Wales for England. In proportion to the area of land, the natives of Australia (126) were fewer in number than the Maoris of New Zealand. Nor do they seem to have been such highly organized people. When Cook and his men sighted the land, it was described by Banks (a scientist on the expedition) as: "gentle sloping hills which had the appearance of the highest

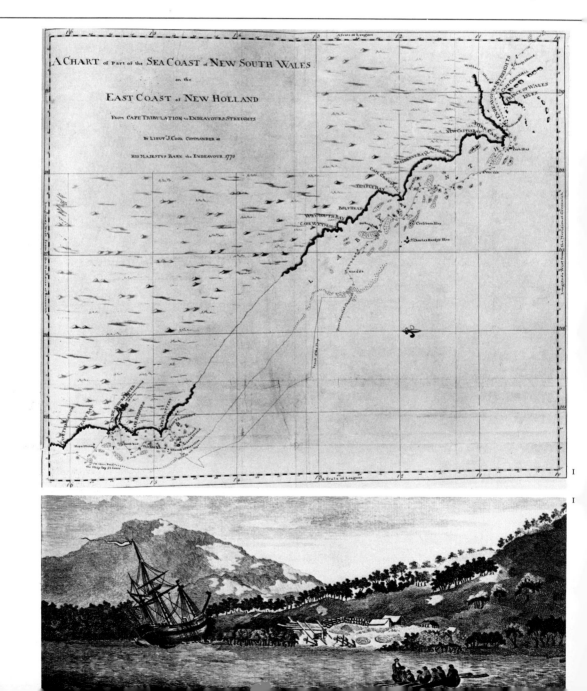

A CHART of Part of the SEA COAST of NEW SOUTH WALES on the EAST COAST of NEW HOLLAND FROM CAPE TRIBULATION to ENDEAVOURS STREIGHTS By LIEUT J. COOK COMMANDER of HIS MAJESTYS BARK the ENDEAVOUR 1770

fertility; every hill seemed to be cloth'd with trees of no mean size; at noon smoke was seen a little way inland and in the evening several more." Later, however, Banks said: "The country, though in general well enough clothed, appeared in some places bare. It resembled in my imagination the back of a lean cow, covered in general with long hair, but nevertheless where her scraggy hip bones have stuck out farther than they ought, accidental rubs and knocks have entirely bared them of their share of covering." Such was the way Australia appeared to her European discoverers. Small wonder that, initially, the English government decided to use the country as a site for a penal colony. The country did not have much appeal to other settlers at that time. Australia never exercized the same hold on contemporary imagination as the New World had, a century and a half before.

126 124 125

127

Dissemination of the knowledge of the exact outline of Australia was slow, as one can see from these two maps. The first by Peter Goos (128) dates from *c.* 1660–9, and the second by Charles de Brosses from 1756 (131). It was even longer before the interior was properly explored—another century, in fact.

Possibly the most famous, or notorious, expedition was that of Robert O'Hara Burke and William J. Wills that set out from Royal Park, Melbourne, in August, 1860. These two men planned to cross the whole of central Australia from south to north (129). Burke and Wills were chosen for the task by the Royal Society of Melbourne, and the Victoria government put up £6,000 to finance the expedition. Six camels were apparently bought from a local circus, and another twenty-four were shipped across from India. So much surplus equipment was accumulated that

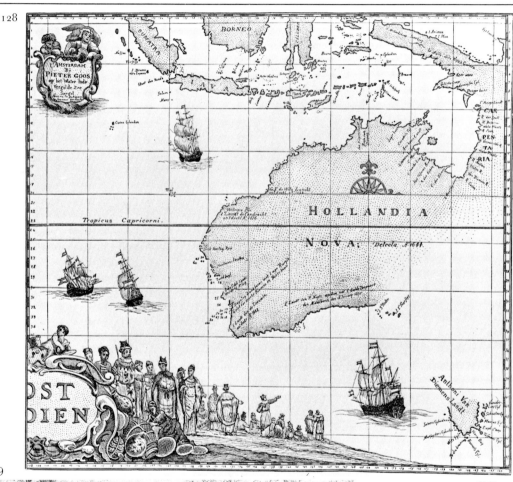

128

129

13

some of it had to be sold off before the expedition could start, Burke, Wills, and King, a third member of the party, pushed on and reached the sea at the Gulf of Carpentaria. On the way back, by a series of almost unbelievable coincidences and misunderstandings, the project came to grief. The men were reduced to living on fish and freshwater mussels, and seeds from plants like the nardoo (130). The expedition was doomed. Burke died first (132), but

Wills did not long survive him. Only King lived to tell the tale. A public funeral was held in their memory in Melbourne (133). It is sad to think that determined action on behalf of the authorities might well have saved the day and the lives of the two explorers. Tragically, a relief expedition had been to their last camp only a few days before they themselves arrived, but failed to make contact. So it was that the little party was doomed.

61

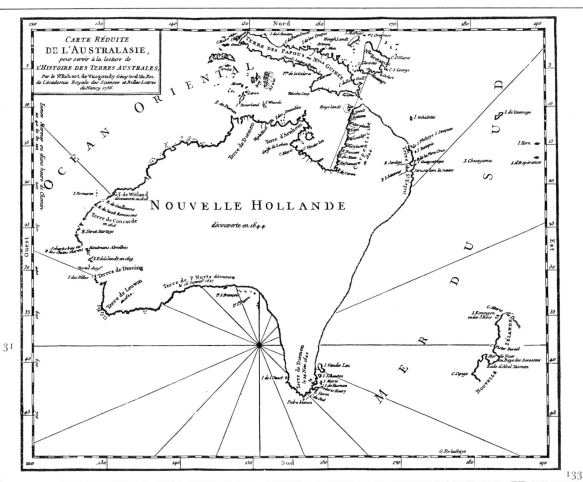

31

133

CHAPTER SIX

THE PACIFIC EXPLORERS

LIKE MANY GREAT DISCOVERIES, in many areas of human progress, the discovery of the Pacific Ocean was a matter of chance. When Christopher Columbus set out to sail across the Atlantic to find a new route to the East, he had no idea that the vast continent of America stood in his way. He had even less of an idea that there was yet another ocean between that continent and his destination. But when Balboa looked down on the Pacific and Magellan sailed across it, the discovery of the Pacific Ocean was an accomplished fact. For the next two hundred years its existence was taken for granted. Few people ever imagined that it would be systematically explored. It was simply a natural obstacle to be crossed in pursuing commerce between East and West. Eventually, though rather late in the day, the French showed an interest in exploring the Pacific. Otherwise, the Dutch, Spanish, and Portuguese were interested in it only because of their various possessions in the East Indies or their trade across it. In fact, one wonders when it would ever have been systematically charted had not Cook been sent to find a southern continent which he believed to be nonexistent.

The idea of a great southern continent had long existed. Certain geographers felt that there must surely be a large land mass somewhere in the south, to "balance" all the land in the Northern Hemisphere. This was a tradition of long standing which lasted well into the eighteenth century. In England, one of its most forceful champions was Alexander Dalrymple, and when he was refused command of a voyage of discovery by the Admiralty, Cook was nominated in his place. In his three successive voyages, Cook discovered the Pacific, and in the fullest sense of the term.

The life and people of the Pacific islands seem to have completely captured his imagination, and we can well imagine how this tropical paradise must have first appeared to Cook and his men. When Banks first set eyes on Tahiti, on the first voyage, he described it as "the truest picture of an arcadia the imagination can form." But more than that, Cook seems to have had a deep understanding of, and feeling for, the natives. For a man brought up in a remote English village in the North Riding of Yorkshire, he had a remarkable sympathy for an alien point of view: "It is impossible for them [the natives] to know our real design. We enter their ports and attempt to land in a peaceable manner. If this succeeds all is well: if not we land nevertheless and maintain our footing by the superiority of our firearms. In what other light can they first look upon us but as invaders of their country?"

Of course, this did not alter the fact that they were, to all intents and purposes, invaders. Yet their whole approach was different from that of the early European ventures among native populations. By the late eighteenth century there was a love of exploration for its own sake—as witness the botanists, naturalists, and artists who accompanied Cook. The following extract from Cook's journal should be read in this light: "As we have not only ascertained the extent and situation of these islands but added several new ones and explored the whole, I think we have obtained a right to name them, and shall for the future distinguish them under the name of the New Hebrides." There were other implications, however, for at the time prestige and empire mattered very much to governments and persons in authority. Cook seems to have accepted this without question, and faithfully planted the English flag at every point, to stake an official claim to the new territories. But the fact that some British officials regarded the discovery of Australia as "compensation" for the loss of the American colonies, shows how far they thought in imperial terms. In purely material terms, however, there could be no comparison between America and Australia at the time. Australia simply represented so many more square miles of empty territory to be painted pink one day

on the British map of the world's surface.

The Pacific was virtually the last area of the globe to confront Western man with new peoples, new cultures, and a completely new world of romantic speculation. Perhaps one day outer space will replace it, but at present the sunny tropical island in the Pacific is still the last bastion of the escapist. The charting of the Pacific meant the end of the real voyages of discovery. Later events—the races to the North and South Poles, the winning of the American West, the opening up of Africa, or the mapping of the Australian continent—required a different kind of pioneer. These men were no less courageous, but there were no more leaps into the great and totally unknown to be made. They were explorers, rather than discoverers. Of course, this did not prevent people from believing all sorts of things, but as far as man's experience of his global environment was concerned, the last piece in the structure was put in place in the closing years of the eighteenth century. Since then, the explorers have set out not to find what is there, but to study in detail what they already know is there. Science followed in the wake of adventure.

Although Balboa was the first European to sight the Pacific Ocean, Magellan was the first to sail on it, in his ship *Victoria*. Magellan was killed by natives on the Island of Mactan in 1521 (134), and after this, there was a lull of more than fifty years before any more concerted efforts were made in this direction, and Sir Francis Drake circumnavigated the world in 1577. This portrait of Drake, dated about 1580, shows a globe in the background (136).

More than a century was to pass before the Dutchman, Abel Tasman, began to explore Australasia, and met the Maoris of New Zealand. This engraving (137) shows a Maori sailing vessel and canoes, and natives swimming out from the beach to welcome the Dutch ships with gifts of fruit. In addition to New Zealand and Tasmania (or Van Diemen's Land as it was first called), Tasman discovered the Friendly Islands and Fiji.

INSVLA MATHAN.

Victoria

The most remarkable Transactions of Lord ANSON's Voyage round the World

134

135

The eighteenth century witnessed a more determined exploration of the Pacific. The British admiral, Lord George Anson (1697–1762), navigated the world, and scenes from his voyages are shown here (135). In 1785 the French navigator, Comte de la Pérouse (Jean François de Galaup) was commissioned by Louis XVI to go to the Pacific, but he was assassinated in Melanesia three years later. This illustrated commemorative chart (138) links his name with that of Captain James Cook, the greatest South Pacific explorer. In fact, all three of Cook's principal voyages had been completed at least five years before La Pérouse set sail. Cook's first voyage (1768–71) took him around the Horn and the Cape of Good Hope; his second (1772–5) led him toward the South Pole and around the world; his third and last (1776–80) took him to the Pacific, where Hawaiian natives killed him.

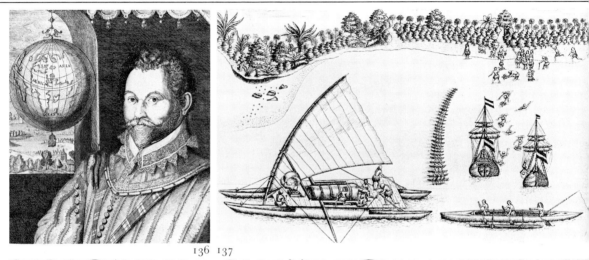

136 137

66 The Friendly Islands, or Tonga Islands as they are more commonly known, were another of Cook's ports of call. This portrait of Cook (141) was painted by John Webber, and hangs in the National Portrait Gallery in London. Cook's ship was the *Resolution*, pictured on a calm sea in this engraving (140). The king of Tonga at the time of Cook's visit was Poulaho, pictured here (139) in a traditional feathered headdress. This illustration first appeared in an early edition of Cook's *Voyages*. Figure (144) shows Poulaho entertaining Captain Cook and his officers with a display of native dancing. Cook's ships lie at anchor a few hundred yards offshore, watched by dozens of curious native fishermen. The native drink was an alcoholic beverage called *kava*, prepared from the roots of a local shrub, and drunk from shallow dishes. This engraving from Cook's *Voyages* (142) shows Poulaho being served the drink. Figure

139

140

141

142

(143) shows Cook landing from a small boat at Middleburgh, another of the Friendly Islands. The natives on the left are bringing gifts.

In 1789 Captain William Bligh of the *Bounty* was cast adrift off the Tonga Islands with eighteen men in a twenty-three-foot open boat with few provisions and no chart. The *Bounty* had been sent to Tahiti in 1787 to collect breadfruit plants, which it was hoped could be cultivated in the West Indies. After the famous mutiny, the mutineers returned to Tahiti, where some were later recaptured and shipped back to England to stand trial. Others sailed on to Pitcairn Island, where they lived undisturbed for twenty years. Bligh meanwhile accomplished a most extraordinary feat. He sailed some 3,600 miles in his open boat, in forty-one days, to the Dutch island of Timor. He was subsequently appointed governor of New South Wales, but was later dismissed.

143

144

Tahiti was discovered by Captain Samuel Wallis. Wallis returned to England on 20th May, 1768, after a voyage of circumnavigation in the *Dolphin* that had lasted almost two years. This was only three months before Cook set sail in the *Endeavour*, and information about the island was to prove of immense value to him. Wallis called the island George Island, after King George III, but this name did not stick; its original name of Tahiti, or Otaheite, has always been the one most commonly used. Whether or not the island was formally surrendered to Wallis by the then queen, Oberea (or Purea), as depicted here (145), is a moot point. However, relations between Wallis and the queen were friendly, and many gifts were exchanged between them (146). When Cook visited the island later, he found Queen Purea's authority disputed, and when he put into Tahiti on his second voyage, she had been

145

146

147

I

deposed and would not come to see him since she had no gifts to offer. From what we read in Cook's own account, it is quite likely that the Tahitians genuinely liked the English, and that leave-takings were sad affairs (149). The English were not the only Europeans to visit the island, however, and not all visitors were on such good terms. With difficulties of languages and customs, misunderstandings easily arose, and the natives could react violently. Wallis himself had such an experience (150). Cook arrived in Matavai Bay, Tahiti, on 13th April, 1769. He was at once surrounded by canoes carrying breadfruit, bananas, and coconuts (147). Cook had taken four of Wallis' men with him, and the natives recognized them. Cook soon set about charting the island with his usual skill and accuracy. The map which he prepared, dated 1769, is reproduced below (148).

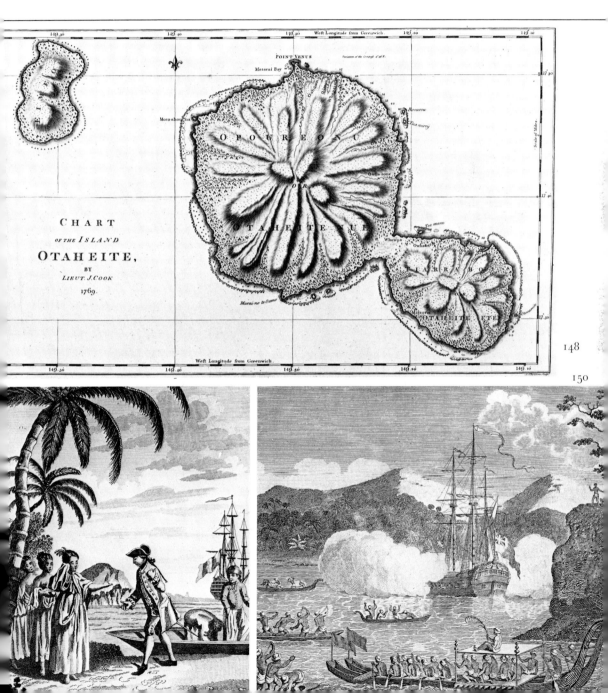

148

150

Ostensibly the object of Cook's first visit to Tahiti (151) was to observe the transit of Venus forecast for 3rd June, 1769. However, he also had a secret Admiralty commission to try to locate the fabled Great South Land, which Cook himself was sure did not exist. The supposed secret commission was the talk of London on the eve of Cook's departure. On his return from his first voyage in 1771 the Admiralty were so delighted with his work that they were reluctant to let him return to routine Naval service, and plans were soon laid for a second voyage. This time William Hodges sailed with the expedition as official artist, and he did many drawings and paintings of war canoes when he arrived in Tahiti, such as this (152). Cook had insisted that this time there should be two ships, and his wishes

151

152

15

were respected, The *Marquis of Granby* and the *Marquis of Rockingham*—renamed *Resolution* and *Adventure*—were duly fitted out. They are seen here at Tahiti (153), which was sighted on 15th August, 1773. Cook anchored first in Vaitepiha Bay, but ten days later moved on to Matavai Bay, where he had previously anchored in *Endeavour*. The natives renewed their acquaintance with Cook, presents were exchanged (154), and new friendships made (155). Cook then left Tahiti and sailed on to New Zealand and into the Antarctic. By the spring of 1774 he was heading north again to Tonga and the Marquesas Islands. He then returned to Tahiti on 22nd April. *Resolution* sailed again on 15th May for Huahine (156), where special entertainments were put on for the visitors.

154

155

As soon as Cook arrived in Tahiti, the natives flocked to see him (157), and the friendly contact established earlier remained much the same—despite one or two minor incidents which occurred from time to time. On his first voyage he was eager to chart the island, which he did in five days with Banks as companion. At Mahaiatea they saw the *marai*, or sacred place, which is the largest of its kind in Polynesia, and whose ruins are still visible today. Cook saw several signs of sacrifice of dogs and pigs but no trace of human sacrifice. He did, however, witness a human sacrifice on his third voyage (158), though such sacrifices were rare; the victims were generally criminals who were killed while asleep. Funerary customs on Tahiti were elaborate and excited the interest of several members of Cook's party on

157

158

15

more than one occasion (159). The breadfruit tree can be seen in this illustration. As we have already seen, it was the breadfruit that attracted Bligh of the *Bounty* to Tahiti.

Because of the fertility of Tahiti, the natives were free to devote much of their time to pastimes such as dancing (160), although this also had great ceremonial significance. Cook also described what appears to have been surfing, which would disprove the claim that the sport originated in Hawaii. The characteristic houses of Tahiti also attracted the attention of Europeans. Figure (161) below shows the house of a chief, standing in a small enclosed area where the women cooked, and undertook other domestic duties. Figure (162) is a pencil sketch showing a "long house." The house is little more than a high roof on posts.

160

161

162

After leaving Easter Island (163) and Tahiti on his second voyage, Cook set out to explore the maze of islands which lay to the west. Bougainville had visited these in 1768 and named them the Great Cyclades. The island of Maewo, which Bougainville christened Aurora Island, was sighted by Cook on 17th July, 1774, and for the next few days he cruised among the islands of the archipelago. On 22nd July he anchored at Mallicolo (165).

Cook eventually named these islands the New Hebrides. Attempts at landing at Mallicolo, and later at Erromanga, both proved unsuccessful, but eventually at Tanna (166) Cook was able to trade with the natives, and take fresh provisions on board ship.

On his third voyage, Cook discovered a group of islands. This was in March, 1777, while he was sailing northeast from New Zealand to Tahiti. These islands are now

163

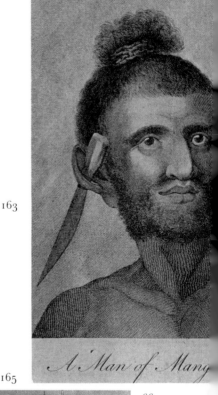

A Man of Mang

165

166

known as the Cook Islands, and among them are Manala, a native of which is shown here (164), and Atiu. It was impossible to land, however, because both islands were encircled by dangerous reefs, but a canoe reached the shore. Cook set off for Tonga because the winds were against a passage to Tahiti. The hard Naval captain now seemed to have taken a short vacation. He spent valuable time cruising through the islands, making long stops in the Haapai group (168), where he was entertained as a chief with singing, dancing, wrestling, and mock fights. After twelve weeks spent in this way, Cook voyaged on to Tahiti, and then to one of the objects of his mission, to see whether a northwest passage was feasible. On the way, he discovered the Hawaiian Islands — or Sandwich Islands as he named them. A burial place is shown here (167). He was to have reason to regret this discovery.

167

164

On 18th January, 1778, Cook sighted the two most western islands of the Sandwich, or Hawaiian, group (171), Eneeheeou and Atoui, known today as Niihau and Kauai. However, it was only on the return trip, having sailed across the Arctic Circle and back, that Cook saw Maui, the second largest of the islands, and Hawaii itself. On 16th January, 1779, after much searching, a suitable anchorage was seen in Kealakekua Bay, where there were two villages, Kekua and Kavarua (169). The first reception was overwhelming (170). It later became obvious that the natives (172, 173) regarded Cook as an incarnation of Lono, the god of peace, happiness, and agriculture, whose return to the islands had been expected at this time. Cook was unaware that he had been deified, although he realized that it was

169

170

171

vital for him to keep up appearances. Soon Kalaniopu, King of Hawaii, arrived; he treated Cook with great respect, taking off his cloak and helmet of red and yellow feathers and putting them on Cook. However, the strain of feeding two shiploads of men soon began to tell on the islanders' resources, and it was with undisguised joy that they learned of Cook's intended departure on 4th February. A great crowd saw him off. However, four days later the foremast of *Resolution* was so badly damaged in a gale that Cook decided to return to Kealakekua Bay to repair it. This time relations with the natives deteriorated rapidly, and at 8 A.M. on Sunday, 14th February, 1779, Cook was killed in a fracas while attempting to take Kalaniopu back to *Resolution* as a hostage (174).

77

172

173

174

CHAPTER SEVEN

THE ARCTIC

ON 7TH JUNE, 1576, Martin Frobisher sailed from England to North America to seek a northwest passage to the East. On 26th July, north of Newfoundland, he passed a cape which he named Queen Elizabeth's Foreland. He found another cape still farther north, but as the wind prevented him from rounding it, he passed instead between the two headlands. Frobisher had entered a bay, but he was convinced that he had America on his left and Asia on his right. Since autumn weather was gathering, Frobisher sailed back across the Atlantic to England, where he arrived on 2nd October. He had brought samples of stone back with him, and it was believed that the stone was gold-bearing ore. Frobisher was therefore commissioned to sail back again the following year, "only for the searching of the ore, and to defer the further discovery of the passage until another time." He returned to the bay which bears his name, and brought back large supplies of the ore, which was pronounced to "show of great profit and wealth." A new voyage was financed for the following year, but this third expedition seemed ill-fated. The ships had a very rough passage, and the ore they brought back turned out to be valueless. Frobisher temporarily fell out of grace, and another seven years elapsed before any new effort was made in north-westerly directions.

In 1585, John Davis received a charter from Queen Elizabeth I for the "search and discoverie of the North West Passage to China." This was the first of three voyages he was to make to the Arctic. He made no great discoveries, and certainly did not discover the Northwest Passage, but he did invaluable work in making more of the North American coastline known to the world at large. Possibly his most important achievement (though he did not know it) was to locate the entrance to Hudson Strait.

Henry Hudson, the next great Arctic explorer, was already a grandfather when he embarked on what was to be his last voyage in 1609. He had previously concerned himself with the Northeast Passage, working for the Muscovy Company and the Dutch East India Company. On his return to England, a consortium of Englishmen commissioned him to sail in search of the Northwest Passage. Hudson carefully navigated his way through the terrifying strait which bears his name, and into the great bay which he firmly believed to be the Pacific. Unfortunately for him, this was not the case, and his crew mutinied and cast him adrift in a boat.

Later exploration was carried out by Sir Thomas Button, but it was the combined work of Robert Bylot and William Baffin which eventually found the real entrance to the Northwest Passage at Lancaster Sound. Again, the importance of the discovery was not realized at the time; Baffin thought that he had merely come across another inlet, and not a strait: "Our hope of a passage began to lessen every day." When Baffin retired from the scene, a long period elapsed before interest turned once more to the Arctic—a period of more than two hundred years.

In 1818, the British Admiralty took advantage of the peace after the Napoleonic wars to send two expeditions to the Arctic. John Ross and William E. Parry went to Baffin Bay and the hoped-for Northwest Passage, and David Buchan and John Franklin were directed to sail to the North Pole and then, if possible, to the Bering Strait. Buchan almost wrecked his ship off Spitsbergen, and had to return, escorted by Franklin. Ross made a useful survey of Baffin Bay, but erroneously thought that Jones and Lancaster sounds were bays only, offering no exit to shipping. Parry was then put in charge of another expedition to Lancaster Sound, and at the same time an overland expedition was sent to survey the coast west of Hudson Bay. This part of the venture was entrusted to Franklin.

Franklin's career was part of an interesting tradition of exploration. He was a pupil of Matthew Flinders, who was himself a pupil of Bligh of *Bounty* fame. Bligh had been Cook's sailing master, and it was to another of Cook's colleagues—Joseph Banks—that Franklin owed his appointment. For three years he endured great hardship in Canada, although to all intents and purposes the voyage was a disaster. Franklin himself survived to lead another expedition to the Arctic, but he disappeared without trace in 1845, and despite several attempts at rescue, no one was able to find him.

Meanwhile, Parry was making his attempt on the Northwest Passage, with the prospect of a reward of £10,000 if he were successful. As it happened, he failed, but he proved himself to be the most careful and successful of Arctic sailors. His record for the farthest north point reached by man stayed unbroken for forty-eight years. He lived long enough to learn that Robert John McClure made the Northwest Passage by walking across the ice stream between Banks Land and Melville Island.

After Franklin and Parry it was the turn of Ross, now a veteran of over fifty years of age, to go on an Arctic expedition. He was financed by Felix Booth, a wealthy Londoner; he set out in 1839. During the course of this voyage, which lasted four years, James Clark Ross located the North Magnetic Pole in the Isthmus of Boothia, named after his patron.

Much remained to be done, however, and many fine men were to perish in the process. Ultimately the Pole itself was reached, and the Northwest Passage navigated—the latter only in the early years of the present century.

Arctic exploration really began with the search for a Northwest Passage to the Far East. In 1576 Martin Frobisher was commissioned by the Muscovy Company of England to look for such a passage. He set out on 7th June of that year, sighting Greenland (177), and naming Frobisher Bay after himself in North America. Meanwhile the Dutchman, Willem Barents, had been attempting to find a Northwest Passage (175), and on his third voyage in 1596 (178) he managed to reach Novaya Zemlya (176). Tragically, the ship was locked fast in the endless ice, and the following year he and the other members of the expedition died of cold and starvation. His winter quarters were discovered generations later in 1871, and part of his historic journal in 1875.

Another explorer of early days, Henry

176

175

177 178

Hudson, gave his name to Hudson Bay and Hudson Strait (179), but he also perished, in the winter of 1610–11, having been left to his fate by his mutinous crew. Nearly 150 years later, men had little more knowledge of this part of the world. This map, which was first published in 1748, is a good example of contemporary knowledge at that date (180). Although much of the region had been ex-plored, and names given to its rivers, lakes, and bays, navigation and charting were still inaccurate sciences. Unsuitable ships and ignorance of the region combined to hold up progress. Indeed, not until Roald Amundsen made his voyage of 1903–5 did a ship finally make the complete voyage through the Northwest Passage. Amundsen's voyage was one of the last milestones of exploration.

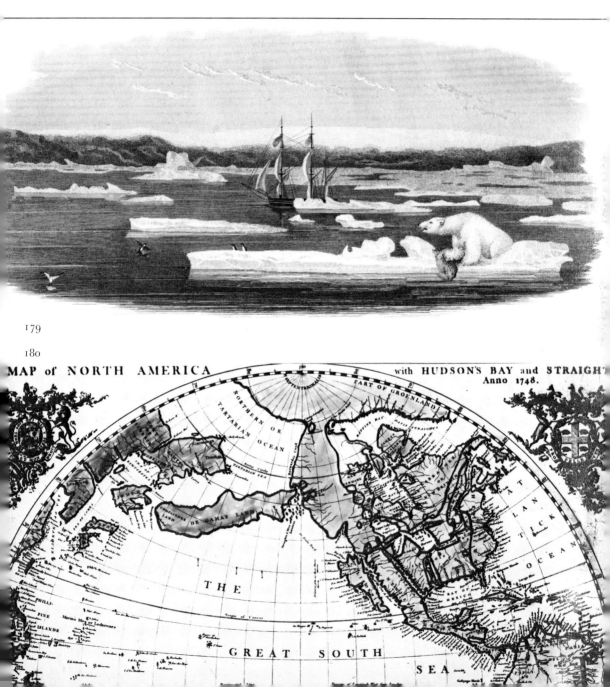

179

180

MAP of NORTH AMERICA with HUDSON'S BAY and STRAIGHT
Anno 1748.

This Russian map of 1763 (181) shows that the Russians were still uncertain about the exact coastline of the northern part of their country. They were even more uncertain about the coast of Alaska, except for the small section opposite the Bering Strait (see upper right segment of the map). The Bering Strait had been first discovered in 1648 by the Russian, Simon Dezhneff, but it was not navigated until 1728. The first man to do this was the Dane, Vitus Bering, who gave his name to the strait. Bering also explored Alaska, and the Russians settled it in 1744. In 1867, however, the territory was sold to the United States of America for the relatively small sum of $7,200,000.

Russia had previously settled the Kamchatka Peninsula (see centre right of the map)

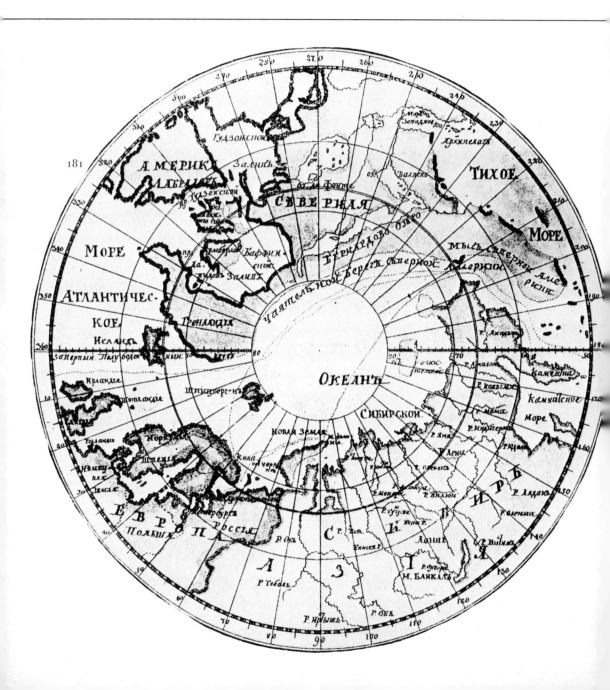

in 1706. By then the peninsula was already valued by the Russians for its furs and fishing. Even today it crab meat is probably the most famous product associated with the area. We see a family of natives in (182) and in (183, 186) one of the chief means of transportation—dog sledges Ships are seen in the port of St. Peter and St. Paul (185) and an early view of Bolcheretzk, the chief town, is given in 184.

In their early years, these settlements were extremely primitive, and gave their inhabitants only a subsistence living. Communications with the outside world were spasmodic and unreliable, and the long winters often brought a good deal of hardship in relation to living conditions, matters of diet, and general health, all of which placed a heavy strain on community life.

182

183

184

185 186 (*bottom*)

Between the years 1585 and 1587, the English sailor John Davis explored the coasts of Greenland and Labrador, and reached 72° 41′ N. In 1616, William Baffin exceeded this, when he reached 72° 45′ N, but Arctic exploration did not really get under way again until the nineteenth century. In 1818 a British Polar expedition set out under the command of W. E. Parry, with John Ross, David Buchan,

and John Franklin, in command of the ships. Their vessels are illustrated below—the *Alexander* (187), *Isabella* (188), *Dorothea* (189), and *Trent* (190) respectively.

At one point, the boats of Franklin's ship were attacked by a herd of walrus, which the crew eventually fought off with such weapons as came to hand (193). At times it was not too difficult to cut a passage through the ice, but

ALEXANDER, 250 Tons, 33 Men. Lieut. Wⁿ EDWᵈ PARRY, Commander.

187

ISABELLA, 382 Tons, 47 Men. Captain JOHN ROSS.

188

DOROTHEA, 370 Tons, 47 Men. Captain DAVID BUCHAN.

189

TRENT, 250 Tons, 33 Men. Lieut. Jⁿ FRANKLIN, Comm

190

191

be imagined from this scene (191),
the risks were great: at one moment, two of the
ships were almost crushed by the tremendous
pressures of ice floes weighing thousands of
tons (194).

In Prince Regent's Bay contact was made
with the natives, as illustrated in this picture
later presented to Captain Ross (194). The
contact seems to have been fairly friendly on
this occasion, but it was not always so, as an
expedition of ten years later discovered to its
cost, when Eskimos swarmed in an attack on
the strange visitors (195). On this expedition
Parry reached Lancaster Sound, which he
crossed, and named the Parry Islands at 114°
W, in the year 1820, in the tradition of many
explorers before him who had named their
discoveries after themselves.

192

3

194

195

Sir James Clark Ross (1800–62) sailed with his uncle, Sir John Ross, on the famous Felix-Booth expedition of 1829, an expedition which was to last four years. This portrait of Sir James Clark Ross hangs in the National Maritime Museum, London (196). His uncle had accompanied Parry on the 1818 expedition. This time, John Ross was in command.

The expedition set sail from London on 23rd May, 1829. Here we see the two ships, decked in flags, passing slowly down the River Thames from Woolwich Docks, cheered by large crowds and a flotilla of small boats (198). The expedition took with it one of the same ships, the *Isabella* (197), which John Ross had commanded on the 1818 venture. The other ship

196

198

197

was the *Victory*, seen here in the port named after Felix (199). When disaster struck the *Victory* its crew were fortunately saved by the *Isabella*, an incident recorded by Ross himself in this sketch (200).

Arriving at Fury Beach, North Somerset, the explorers named their headquarters Somerset House. Here (201) is the drawing made of it by Ross himself, and first published in 1834. From this desolate spot they set out for Batty Bay by an overland route. Then, in 1831, two years after leaving London, James Clark Ross became the first man to locate the exact position of the North Magnetic Pole, in the territory which they named the Boothia Peninsula.

199

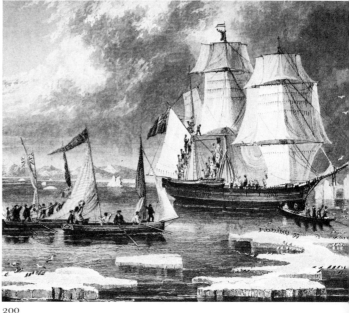

200

201

In 1845, Sir John Franklin (202), who had sailed in the 1818 expedition with Parry, and after whom Port Franklin was named (205), sailed on an expedition with the ships *Erebus* and *Terror* (203) for the Arctic Northwest Passage. He failed to return. After some time, a relief expedition under Sir Edward Belcher was sent to find him in 1852. The ships involved on this occasion were the *Phoenix*, the *Talbot*, and the *Diligence* (204).

Paradoxically, it was on this relief expedition that the existence of a Northwest Passage was determined for once and for all. However, another fifty years were destined to elapse before anyone actually navigated it. The first man to do so was to be Amundsen in the *Gjoa*.

202

203

204

The Belcher expedition, after undertaking an exhaustive search, failed to find Franklin, and returned home to England two years later. In fact, Franklin's ships had been completely trapped in the vast ice floes. There was to be no escape. The crew officers and men abandoned the useless vessels (206), and eventually all perished from scurvy due to vitamin deficiency. Scurvy was a perennial hazard of such expeditions.

In 1859 a commemorative cairn was opened on Victory Point (207), which contained documents relating to Captain F. R. M. Crozier and Captain Fitzjames. Other relics of the Franklin expedition appear in illustrations on page 124.

90 The *Racehorse* was the companion ship to *Carcass* in an expedition commanded by Captain C. J. Phipps (Lord Mulgrave) and Captain Lutwyche to the North Pole in 1800. *Racehorse* is shown here trapped by pack ice (208). Indeed, at one point, both ships were caught in the ice, at 80° 37' N.

Specially designed for their work, explora-

tion ships did not change much in basic design during the course of a hundred years. One can compare these earlier vessels with those of the George S. Nares expedition of 1875, for example. Here are three ships of the Nares expedition: *Valorous* (209) is seen leaving *Alert* (210) and *Discovery* (211).

However, the equipment used by the

209

208 211

210

explorers themselves certainly did improve, especially as more and more experience of Polar conditions was gained. European explorers, especially those who were accustomed to northern climates, were more easily able to adapt to the fierce conditions which prevailed in the Arctic and Antarctic. They could also learn a great deal from the Eskimos they encountered on their journeys (212). One example of what they learned was the use of dogs to haul sledges across the ice and snow (213). Innovations like this made inland exploration more feasible, and reduced the exhaustion and fatigue which overland explorers otherwise experienced, and which was often the cause of their failures.

212

213

The closing years of the nineteenth century saw a great deal of Arctic exploration. By this time, Eskimos often used to act as guides and interpreters for the European voyages. Hans Henrik (214) was a famous Eskimo guide in his day.

Arctic exploration was by no means the preserve of the British. Baron Nils Nordenskjöld (216) was a famous Finnish explorer. He had studied mineralogy and mining and made several expeditions to Spitsbergen, where he made valuable geological discoveries. In 1878 he made a voyage in the *Vega*, during the course of which he navigated the Northwest Passage (217). In 1883 he made another expedition, this time to Greenland (215).

214

215

216

217

Later Arctic expeditions included those of the *Eira* in 1881 (218) and of Adolphus W. Greely (220) in 1884. But the American, Robert E. Peary (219), was the man who first reached the Pole itself. He had begun his operations in 1886 on the Greenland ice cap. Then, between 1891 and 1896, he made several trips over north Greenland, and in the four years from 1898 to 1902 he explored and charted Ellesmere Land, journeyed around the north coast of Greenland, and reached 84° 17′ N. He spent the winter of 1905 in the Arctic Ocean aboard his ship the *Roosevelt*, during which time he reached 87° 86′ N. Finally, in 1908, he sailed in the *Roosevelt* once again, and reached the Pole on 6th April, 1909.

218

219

220

At the end of the nineteenth century, progress in Polar exploration was being made by leaps and bounds, and conditions were far removed from the early days of European excursions into the frozen north of the sort seen here (221). In 1893 Fridtjof Nansen (222), Norwegian, made one of the most historic Polar voyages of all. He sailed in a specially constructed ship, the *Fram* (223), which was later used by Roald Amundsen. His plan was to allow his ship to be caught in the ice, and let the moving ice float him across the Arctic Ocean, with the chance of passing over the Pole. He then made a dash for the Pole over the ice, and reached 86° 14′ N, but eventually he had to be rescued in the territory of Franz Joseph Land. He is seen here united with the crew of the *Fram* (224), and in a kayak (225). His return to

221

Oslo—or Christiania as it then was called—was an occasion for great national celebrations in 1896 (226). This photograph was taken from a captive balloon.

Curiously enough, a Swede, S. A. Andrée, attempted to reach the Pole by balloon in 1897, but he perished in the attempt. His body was discovered years later in 1930. In 1926 Amundsen flew an airship, the *Norge*, over the Pole, but just two days earlier Richard E. Byrd had already flown over it in an airplane. In 1928 an Italian expedition set out in the *Norge*—renamed the *Italia* for the occasion—and achieved its objective. The airship was unfortunately destroyed on the return trip. Amundsen set out in a seaplane to look for the leader of the expedition, General Umberto Nobile, but was himself never seen again.

222

223

224

225

226

CHAPTER EIGHT

THE ANTARCTIC

THE DISCOVERY OF ANTARCTICA was first inspired by a belief in the existence of a great southern continent. This tradition had its origins in the ancient world. In fact, not until the late eighteenth century was the existence of such a continent finally disproved. Captain Cook wrote: "As to a southern continent, I do not believe any such thing exists, unless in a high latitude." After his first voyage of 1768–71, Cook maintained that his journey "must be allowed to have set aside the most, if not all, the arguments and proofs that have been advanced by different authors to prove that there must be a southern continent—I mean to the northward of 40° for what may lie to the southward of that latitude I know not. Certain it is that we saw no visible signs of land, according to my opinion, neither in our route to the northward, southward or westward, until a few days before we made the coast of New Zealand."

But Alexander Dalrymple, who had wished to lead the expedition, and who believed strongly that such a continent existed, said that, had he been in command, "I would not have come back in ignorance." The following year (1772) he published his ideas about the nature of the continent: "The number of inhabitants in the southern continent is probably more than fifty millions. This is a greater extent than the whole civilized part of Asia, from Turkey to the eastern extremity of China. There is at present no trade from

Europe thither, though the scraps from this table would be sufficient to maintain the power, dominion, and sovereignty of Britain, by employing its manufacturers and ships." Dalrymple was persuasive.

On his second voyage Cook was told specifically to search for a southern continent. If he encountered inhabitants, he was to show them "every kind of civility and regard." Having left Plymouth on 13th July, 1772, the crew saw the first icebergs on 10th December, drifting southward from Capetown. The Antarctic Circle was crossed on 17th January, 1773. By the time Cook reached New Zealand, on 25th March, he had sailed 12,000 miles without sighting land. The Circle was crossed again later that year, after they had spent a summer in the Pacific. Despite the hazards, the fog, and the cold, Cook went on toward Cape Horn and found no continent. A third crossing of the Circle was made on 26th January, 1774, much farther east than on the two previous occasions. Cook reached 71° 10′ S; although the South Pole was still hundreds of miles away, no one had ever been as close to it before. Cook wrote, "I will not say that it was impossible anywhere to get further to the south, but the attempting it would have been a dangerous and rash enterprise, and what I believe no man in my situation would have thought of." He went on: "I who had ambition not only to go further than anyone had been before, but as far as it was possible for man to go, was not sorry at this interruption, as it in some measure relieved us, at least shortened the dangers and hardships inseparable from the navigation of the southern polar regions." Cook's conclusion was that the lands to the south would never be explored, and that if anyone cared to do so, "I shall not envy him the fame of his discovery, but I make bold to declare that the world will derive no benefit from it."

In a sense, Cook was right. It is hard to see what lasting benefit the world has received from the exploration of Antarctica. There were the immediate benefits of a sealing trade and later a whaling trade, but, to begin with, both were temporary booms. The future interest of Antarctica was to lie in another context.

The magnetic poles had been a matter of interest and experiment for several scientists and explorers, and in particular the German, Alexander von Humboldt. It was known that the magnetic poles did not coincide with the geographical poles, but observations had suggested that the magnetic poles were not fixed. Humboldt himself organized a series of magnetic observation stations across Europe and North America. Another German, Karl Friedrich Gauss, demonstrated mathematically that the earth's magnetic field had a definite north–south path. In 1831, James Clark Ross reached the North Magnetic Pole, and was then chosen to lead a British expedition to the South Magnetic Pole. At the same time the United States launched out into exploration proper, and sent Charles Wilkes to the Antarctic.

Both these expeditions, however, were anticipated by a French mission under Dumont d'Urville in September, 1837. Apart from his feats of exploration, Dumont d'Urville's great claim to fame was that he secured the statue of Venus de Milo for the Louvre in Paris. He was not a dedicated Antarctic explorer, but King Louis Philippe of France ordered him to go there. Dumont d'Urville did not succeed in his quest, however, and returned to France. He later died in a railway accident. Wilkes was no more successful, and after surviving two courts-martial, he died, a somewhat eccentric old man. Only Ross had a pleasant retirement, which he interrupted to go in search of Franklin and Crozier in the Arctic in 1848. But one of them reached the South Magnetic Pole.

After this early burst of activity, Antarctic exploration was neglected until the end of the century. People had begun to explore inland—including men like Ernest Shackleton and Robert Scott. But despite the magnificent work they did, the victory was finally won by Roald Amundsen. His description of the event is a rather ironic anticlimax. "The goal was reached, the journey ended. I cannot say—though I know it would sound much more effective —that the object of my life was obtained."

After the rounding of the Cape of Good Hope —seen here is Table Bay (231)—and then Cape Horn by Willem Schouten (228), the unknown frontiers of the South Polar regions were pushed farther and farther back. But Mercator's map of 1538 (227) and Ortelius' atlas of about the same date (232) both show what an immense task lay ahead for future navigators. Both maps assume that Tierra del Fuego was the northern part of a great unknown continent which stretched away to the south. Mercator's map is a reasonably accurate representation of South America, but that of Ortelius mistakes the real shape of the region, although a good deal of exploration had by then been carried out in both coastal and

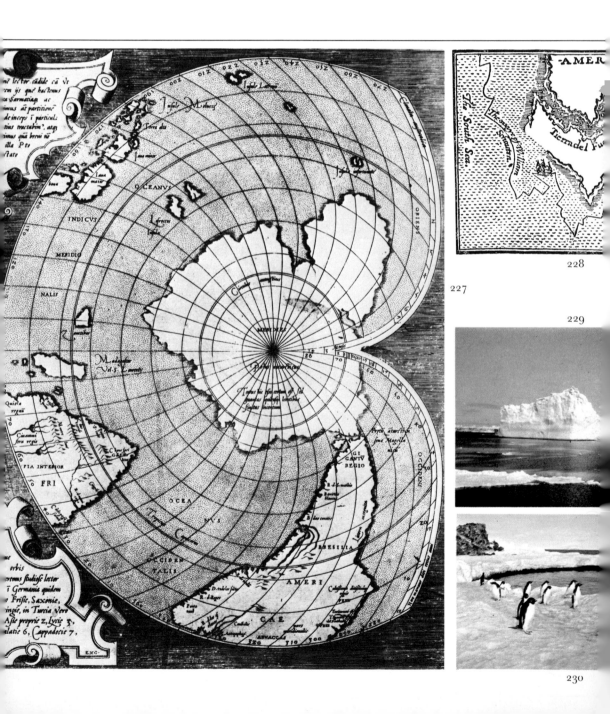

227

228

229

230

inland regions. Almost four hundred years were to pass before the work was finished. The one immediate result of Schouten's voyage was that Tierra del Fuego was shown to be not itself a part of the Polar land mass, but a separate group of islands.

Nearly all of the South Polar continent lies inside the Antarctic Circle, and has an area of some five million square miles. The Antarctic Ocean (229 shows icebergs) is the shallowest of oceans, having an average depth of only 2,000 fathoms. The discovery of the South Pole was, apart from the climbing of Mount Everest, one of the last great adventures left on earth for twentieth-century man. Figure (230) shows Adélie penguins.

231

AMERICAE SIVE NOVI ORBIS, NOVA DESCRIPTIO.

Antarctic exploration can be said to have begun when Captain Cook, on his second voyage, became the first man to cross the Antarctic Circle. This he did on 17th January, 1773 (233). On that day, Cook (235) jubilantly wrote: "A quarter past 11 o'clock we crossed the Antarctic Circle, and are undoubtedly the first and only ship that ever crossed that line." He was to cross it twice more on that same voyage, as can be seen in (233).

He soon turned his ship around, however, and headed northward in search of Kerguelen's Land (234). In fact, it was not until 24th December, 1776, on his third voyage, that he finally located the islands; the following day he anchored in a bay he appropriately named Christmas Harbour (236). Ever in search of the supposed Great South Land, Cook had

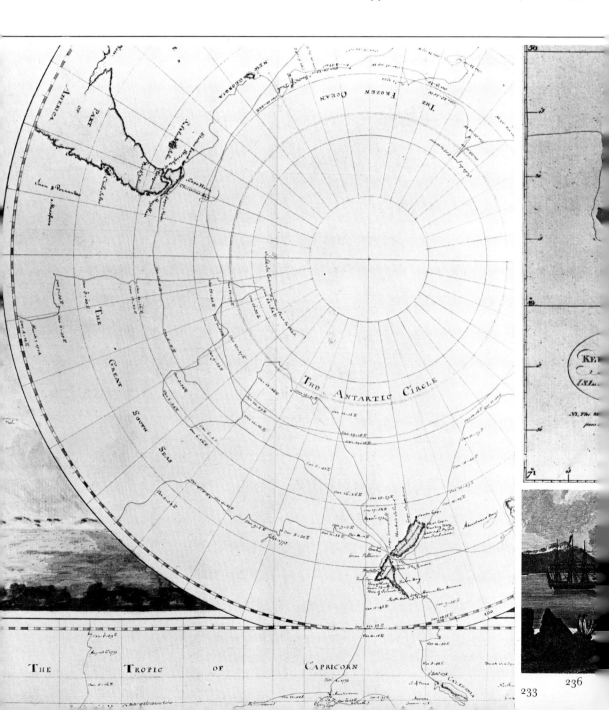

233

236

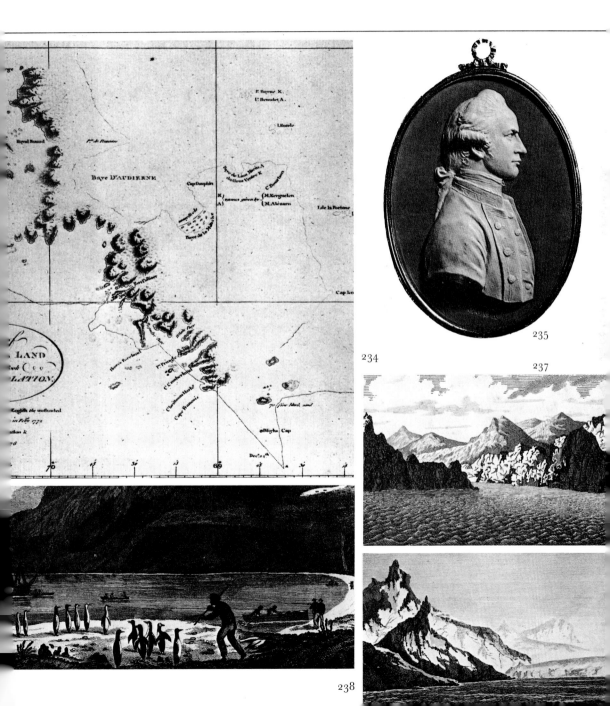

discovered land which he called South Georgia, east of Cape Horn. It proved bleak and barren, and the interior was "not less savage and horrible" than the shore. If this was the great southern continent, then it was "not worth the discovery." Cook took formal possession with a volley of musketry and sailed on. But first he took care to assure himself that it was only an island, and not the elusive continent, about which so much had been written. Here are two views of the coast of this desolate region, with its snowcapped peaks (237, 238). They were first reproduced as engravings in an early edition of Cook's *Voyages*. The bay illustrated in figure (237) was christened Possession Bay. "Thus an idea of a southern continent adopted by M. de Kerguelen vanished before the accurate researches of Captain Cook."

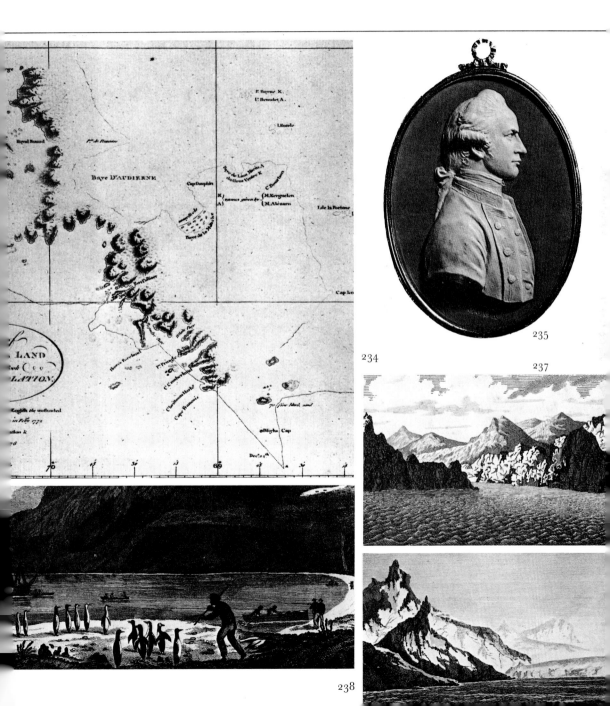

234

235

237

238

The Antarctic Ocean consists of the southern parts of three different oceans: the Pacific, the Atlantic, and the Indian. The peculiar local effect of the sun's light which appears as a pillar in the sky over the sea ice is one that many explorers have seen and discussed. Here is a photograph of this strange phenomenon (239).

Although the sheet ice at the Pole itself is between 1,000 and 2,000 feet thick, there is volcanic activity on the land mass, and occasionally new islands are thrown up. One example was Deception Island, shown here (240). At present Mount Erebus on Ross Island is the only active volcano in the Antarctic region (241). The Antarctic has no

239

240

241

land animals as such, only penguins, seen here against Mount Erebus (242), and whales and seals.

In 1823 the explorer James Weddell reached the sea that now bears his name, but this "sea" is in fact a huge bay. Weddell also gave his name to a kind of seal (243), seen here surfacing at a hole in the ice. A special feature of Ross Island, in addition to its volcano, is its ice caves. Their strange and fantastic formations (244) have an awe-inspiring beauty, which has fascinated all those who have seen them.

Ross Island was named after the English explorer, Sir James Clark Ross, important for his work in the Antarctic regions.

242

243

244

The Ice Islands (245), encountered a few days before Cook crossed the Antarctic Circle, and Tierra del Fuego (248) and Staten Land (247), were visited by Cook on his first voyage. Here (246) is a page of Cook's log book from his first voyage; Cook does not seem to have been averse to lifting whole sections from Banks' journal for the eventual publication of his own *Voyages*. On this page from his second voyage, the one to the South Pole, Cook's signature appears (250).

In 1839 Sir James Clark Ross was placed in command of a British Antarctic expedition sponsored by the Admiralty in London (249). During this expedition, he discovered the Admiralty Mountains, Possession Island,

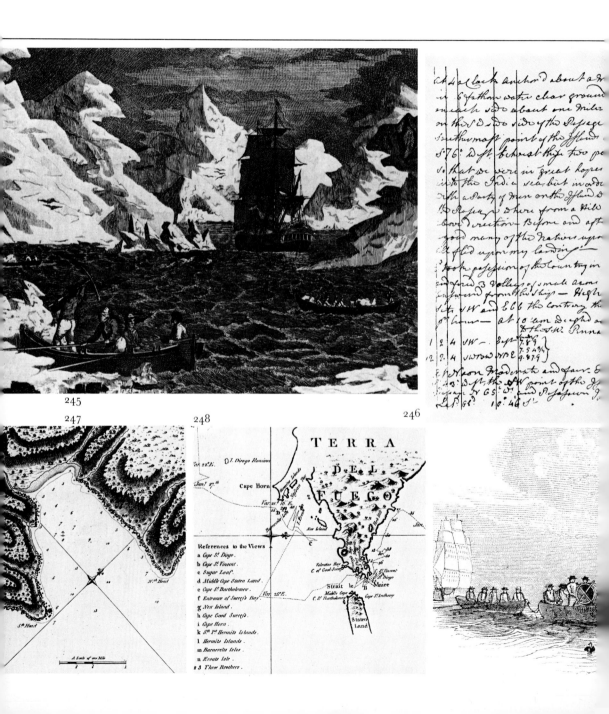

245

247

248

246

Coulman Island, Mount Melbourne, Franklin Island, Mounts Erebus and Terror—named after the ships of the 1845 Franklin Arctic expedition—and Cape Crozier. For those who were forced to spend their Christmas in the Antarctic, seasonal festivities were organized, and on this occasion (251) the patriotic members of the expedition created statues in snow or ice of Queen Victoria and Prince Albert.

Sir James Clark Ross (1800–62) published an account of his discoveries in 1847, under the title *A Voyage in the Southern and Antarctic Regions (1839–43)*. It was a major contribution toward a knowledge of this immense—and inhospitable—region.

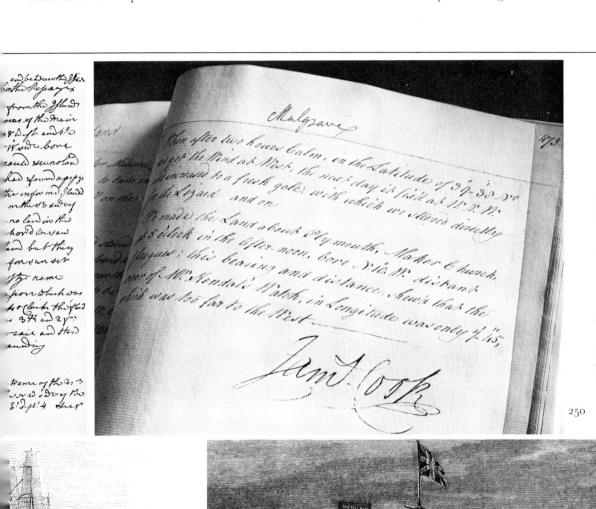

250

249 251

106   In 1901 Robert Scott sailed in the *Discovery*, seen here in winter quarters with Observation Hill in the background (252). A party was landed at the foot of Mount Terror on Ross Island on 22nd January, 1902. The ship then followed the Great Ice Barrier eastward, and in so doing discovered a new territory which was named King Edward VII Land. The crew

members spent the winter in McMurdo Sound, and then made sledge journeys in a southward direction over the barrier ice. Royd's sledge party is seen setting out on reconnaissance to the southwest to Mount Discovery on 10th September, 1902 (253). Scott's base camp at Cape Evans is shown below (254). Figure (255) is a photograph

252

253   254

taken by one of the party, showing Scott and Blissett hauling in seal meat on a snow sled; and figure (257) shows the Southern Cross Hut under construction at Cape Adare.

Scott (256) was finally to reach the Pole himself in 1912, using sledges dragged by hand, one month after Amundsen. But unfortunately he perished while making the return journey. Painfully making his way through the snow and ice, this great explorer at last fell victim to scurvy and to hunger, two of the most common hazards faced by expeditions in these remote and desolate parts. His ship, the *Discovery*, is preserved as a museum on the River Thames, London, together with his log book and its last tragic entries.

255

257

256

Roald Amundsen (258) sailed from Norway aboard the *Fram* in August, 1910, and arrived in the Bay of Whales on the edge of the Great Ice Barrier in January of the following year. He immediately set up his winter quarters, and in October of that year began to make his dash overland for the Pole, which he reached on 16th December, 1911 (259). The dash was made on ice sledges pulled by dogs.

In 1914 Ernest Shackleton, who had discovered the South Magnetic Pole in 1908, left England on the *Endurance* (260), in order to attempt a journey by sledge from the Weddell Sea right across Antarctica to the Ross Sea. The *Endurance* became frozen in ice off the Caird Coast in January, 1915. Desperate

258
259
260

attempts were made by the crew to cut a passage through the ice, as shown in (263), but despite all their efforts the ship was eventually crushed and destroyed in October, 1915, having drifted from 76° 30′ S to 69° S (262). Luckily the crew themselves were rescued, although not without some difficulty. Figure (261) is a typical photograph of one of their camps on the ice. The shovels have been used for clearing a space in the ice; in the background is one of the lifeboats, mounted on runners so that it could be dragged over the ice and used again. With so much physical work to be done, every Polar expedition took a tremendous toll of exhaustion from those who took part in them.

261

262

263

CHAPTER NINE

THE SCIENCE
OF NAVIGATION

FROM THE LATE THIRTEENTH CENTURY (the date of the earliest surviving portulan chart) to the late fifteenth century, charts changed very little. The word "portulan" refers specifically to written sailing instructions. Hence these portulan charts were maps consisting of sailing instructions. The charts were drawn up on the basis of known routes and distances between ports and headlands, all plotted as base points. The distances were measured in miles, not degrees, and the bearings were shown in straight lines corresponding to points of the compass. The coast between the base points was then drawn in with a reasonable accuracy. There were no parallels or medians as on modern maps, and no notice was taken of the fact that the surface of the earth was curved. Moreover, all charts were drawn with the Magnetic North as the vertical.

In a chart of the Mediterranean, for example, the margin of error was not important because the area was in any case fairly small. But when the Portuguese began to push farther and farther south, down the west coast of Africa, they began to need charts showing more detailed information. A regular school of chart makers flourished in Lisbon, helped a good deal by expatriate Genoese. Bartholomew Columbus—Christophers' own brother—worked in Portugal for a time. John II, who took up the mantle of Henry the Navigator, encouraged the mapping and charting of the African coast. At the same time he tried to stop the knowledge from being passed on to foreigners.

Although the basic style of charts remained the same, one important improvement was made at the beginning of the sixteenth century. A single meridian was added—usually that of Cape St. Vincent—with degrees of latitude marked on it. This was still a *magnetic* meridian so that some maps had a second, *geographical*, meridian drawn in. From charts of individual areas, world charts were pieced together. The most ambitious of these was the Spanish *Padrón Real* in Seville, a kind of official compilation of all the discoveries, begun in 1508 at royal command. Portuguese cartographers also worked on this map from time to time.

A time soon came, however, when the portulan method was no longer accurate enough—particularly for sailors making longer voyages of exploration and circumnavigation. World charts could be adequately produced only with the aid of globes and world maps. In practice, this meant abandoning most of the "Ptolemaic system" which had dominated geography for centuries. The Ptolemaic system was really a summary of the geographical knowledge of the ancient world as compiled by Ptolemy of Alexandria (*c.*87–150). In the years around 500 B.C. Pythagorean philosophers demonstrated that the earth was a sphere. Eratosthenes (third century B.C.) worked out its circumference, and in the second century B.C. Hipparchus showed that it revolved around the sun. But when one looks at the thirteenth-century map preserved in Hereford Cathedral in England, one realizes that all this knowledge had long been forgotten. The later discoveries of the Arabs had failed to penetrate the West. Eventually, some of the learning of Islam filtered through Spain into the universities of France and so to the rest of Europe. But it was a long process.

Basically, Ptolemy miscalculated the size of the globe. Also he was wrong about the shape and extent of Asia and the supposed land mass known as *terra australis incognita* in the Southern Hemisphere, which was not disproved until the late eighteenth century. When Diaz and Vasco da Gama sailed around the Cape of Good Hope, they demolished one of the main props of Ptolemaic ideas, and when Magellan and Del Cano circumnavigated the world, they demolished another by showing how large the Pacific was and how small Asia was by comparison. But the main Ptolemaic idea—the sphericity of the earth—could not be abandoned. So at last came the great breakthrough of 1569, when Mercator published his world map at Duisburg, and popularized the idea of map projections.

In addition to maps, other necessary aids to sailors included the compass and a more simple piece of apparatus—the lead and line. These echo two traditions of seamanship which combined to launch the Europeans on their voyages of discovery. First was the Mediterranean tradition based on the use of the compass (supposed to have originated in Amalfi). This involved written sailing instructions, traverse tables, marine charts, and dead reckoning. The other tradition was that of the Atlantic. Less precise sailing instructions were usual—no charts, limited dead reckoning, experience of storms and fogs, tides and timetables, and constant use of the lead and line, particularly when sailing off a new or unknown coast. Europe needed something more. Hence two of the astronomer's instruments were borrowed by navigators—the astrolabe and the quadrant to determine latitude. Later the cross-staff was adopted—also from the astronomers—its advantage over the astrolabe and quadrant was that it used the actual horizon, not an artificial one. Longitude, however, could not be measured until chronometers were perfected in the eighteenth century.

When the voyages of discovery, and particularly the early ones, were made, primitive maps, charts, and navigational instruments could take the ships only so far. They could facilitate their progress only up to a certain point. After that, an expedition had to rely heavily on the staying power of crews and vessels, experience, and that indefinable quality which is a mixture of faith, determination, and the ability to survive in the face of adversity.

This early map (264) was drawn on the Ptolemaic system, the most common system in use in the Western world for almost 1,500 years. The *carta de marear* or *mapa mundi* (world map) of Juan de la Cosa (265) dates from 1500. This is the first surviving chart on which Columbus' discoveries are shown. De la Cosa had sailed with Columbus on his two earlier voyages, and probably also sailed with Vespucci on his voyage of 1499.

Leonardo da Vinci's map of the world showed how rapidly the new understanding of the nature of the globe was beginning to spread. Yet despite the advances of knowledge during the Renaissance, ideas about the exact location of one place to another were still rather

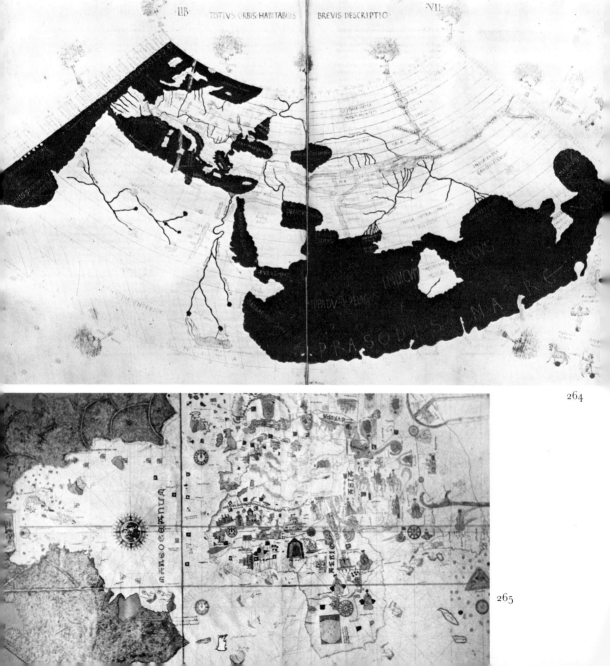

264

265

vague. Johannes Schöner's globe of 1515 (266) is a demonstration of this vagueness. Brazil, for example, is shown as part of the supposed Great South Land instead of South America; the west coast of America is described as *incognita* (unknown). Also, the islands of the Caribbean and of the Indian Ocean and China Sea are poorly conceived,

Schöner's globe carries strange representations of seamonsters, some half-human, reflecting the legends and superstitions of the time. In a famous passage the English poet Edmund Spenser (1552–99) pictured "huge seamonsters, such as living sense dismayed; most ugly shapes and horrible aspects such as Dame Nature herself must fear to see."

The defeat of the Spanish Armada in 1588 (267) showed, probably more vividly than anything else, that times had changed. In this new age of discovery, the huge galleons of Mediterranean origin were entirely unsuited to the new ideas of navigation and the conditions experienced on the open seas. Their vast high sails and high structures made them unsafe for long ocean voyages. They could sometimes be used as convoy ships, but even then they were vulnerable. The wreck of the Spanish Armada in point of fact marked the emergence of the British and Dutch as the two major Naval powers of the future.

It was through the Dutch presence in the Far East that the existence of Australia was made known. Pierre Desceliers' map of 1550 (269) shows a rather romantic impression of

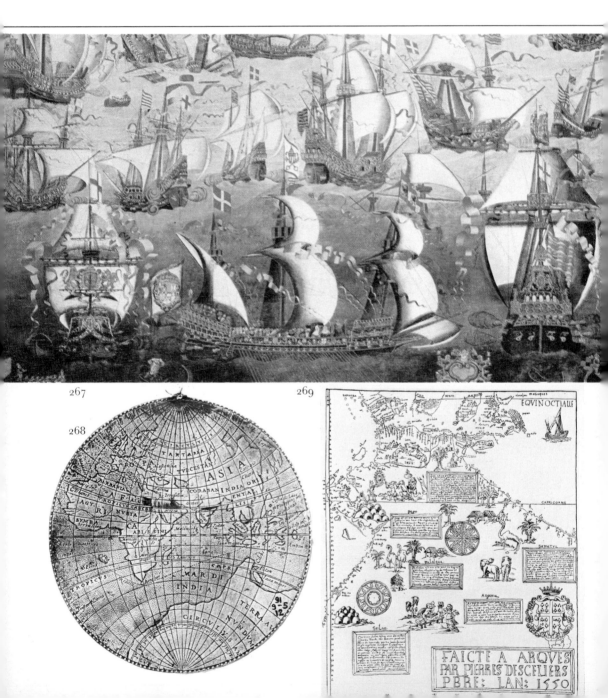

267

268

269

what went on there; for the complete map, see figure (73). The East Indies, on the other hand, were well charted by this time, as this map of 1558 shows (270). In 1577, Drake had circumnavigated the world, as commemorated on this engraved medallion (268). Although Drake realized that there was sea beyond Tierra del Fuego, he did not round Cape Horn but left this to Schouten. On this map (271), published in Antwerp in 1562, Tierra del Fuego is still shown as part of a southern land mass and, despite Schouten's voyage, continued to be shown as such on some maps for almost another century. By 1631 the eastern seaboard of North America was being colonized, and New England (272) was well established. Plymouth Colony had been founded in 1620, and Massachusetts in 1629.

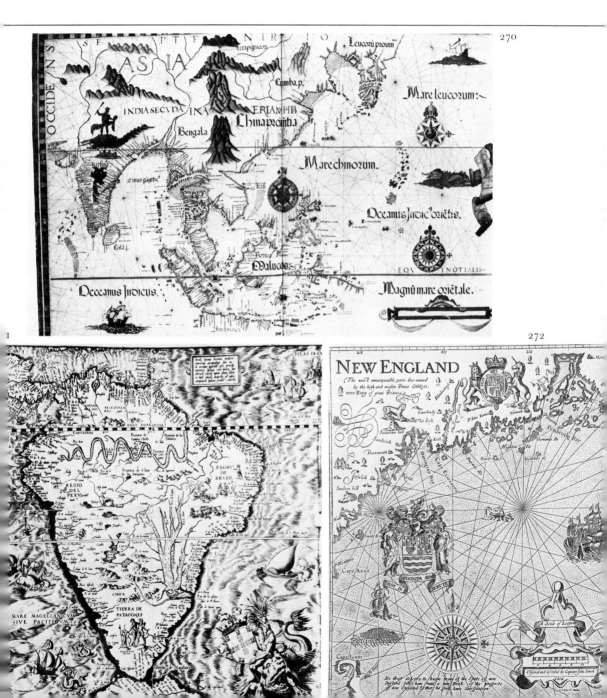

270

1

272

116 Figure (273) shows a chart of North and South America by the Dutchman Pieter Goos, about 1660–70, engraved on vellum. Figure (274) is a map of Canada reproduced from P. Duval's *Géographie Universelle*, also from the second half of the seventeenth century. Although he was the French Geographer Royal, Duval shows in this map that he thought the Ottawa, and not the Niagara, drained Lake Erie to the sea. Father Hennepin did an immense amount to increase knowledge of North America, and although this map of 1683 (275) underestimates the distance from Florida to Canada, it is more accurate in many respects than that of Duval.

Of all the attempts at settlement in the New

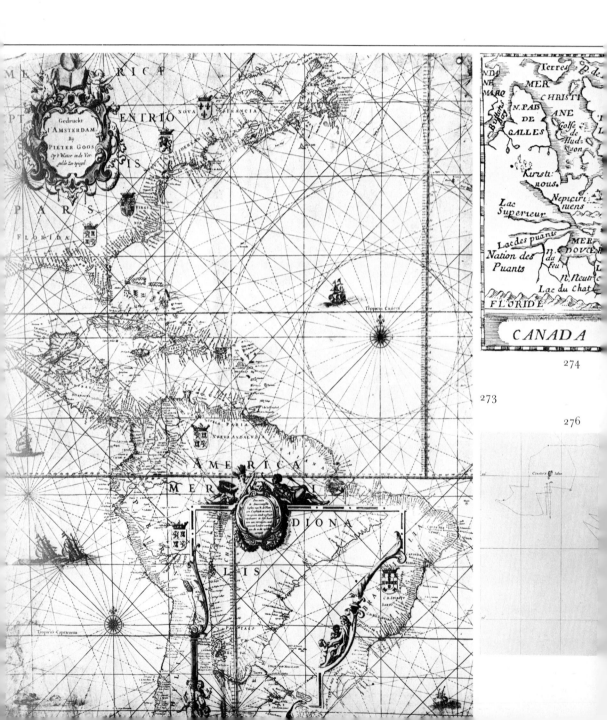

274

273

276

World by the British, that of the Scots at the Isthmus of Panama in 1699 was probably the least likely to have succeeded (277). It was the humid climate of Central America, possibly more than anything else, that proved lethal to the settlers, who were unable to combat disease.

The precise work of Cook is well illustrated by the maps and charts he made during his voyages. The map (276) is from his second voyage, with *Resolution*, when he went across the Antarctic Circle, charting the southwest coast of the Isle of Georgia. Cook is important in the history of exploration, not only as a leader of voyage's of discovery, but as a cartographer of considerable skill.

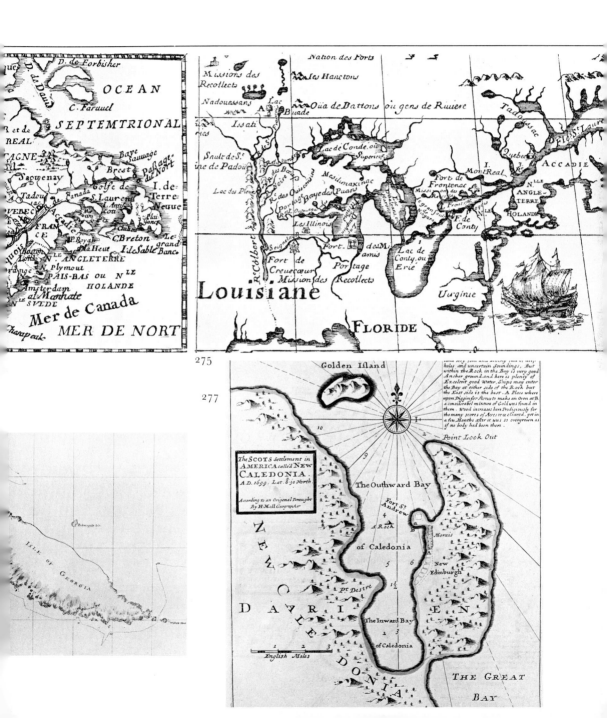

275

277

The main instruments of navigation remained unchanged for centuries. Seen here (278) are an hourglass, a globe, a quadrant, a cross-staff, chart and dividers, astrolabe and cartographers' rulers. The most ancient instrument of astronomic navigation—that is, navigation by the stars—is the astrolabe. This device was of Arabic origin. Figure (281) shows the reverse side of a fifteenth-century astrolabe.

The observer holds the instrument with his thumb through the ring or hangs it up by the ring, and then places it in the vertical plane bounded by the star he is looking at, his eye, and the Pole. In this way the sun, moon, and stars are visible in the axis of the two holes in the moveable bar or allotrope. Latitude can then be calculated from the angle between the vertical and the angle of vision by reading the

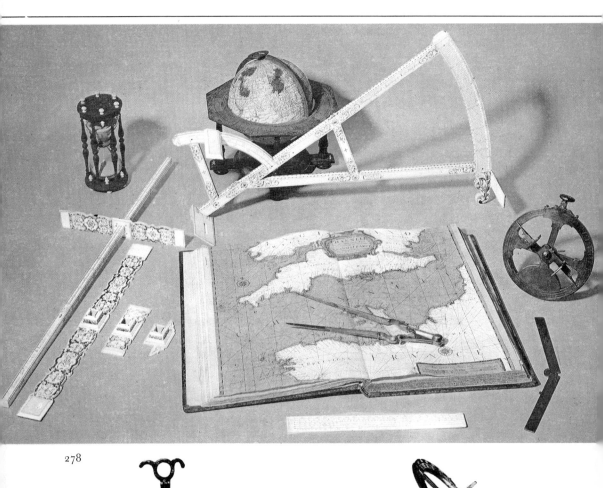

278

279

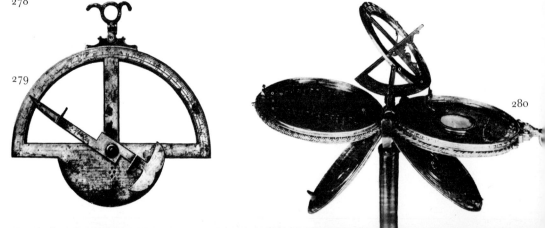

280

gradations on the edge of the disc. The illustration (283) to Père Fournier's *Hydrographie* of 1643 shows the front of an astrolabe. An early seventeenth-century Danish astrolabe is shown also (279).

Drake's exploits gave great impetus to navigation, as was symbolized on a title page to the English edition of Lucas Waghenaer's book, *The Mariners Mirrour* (282), and his

dial or astrolabe (280) of 1569. This fascinating instrument was made for him by Humphrey Cole and was presented to him the year before his expedition to the West Indies. It is made of brass and has seven dials which help to calculate the time of high water, moveable feast days, and the passage of the sun through the zodiac. Drake must have found this ingenious contrivance most useful.

281

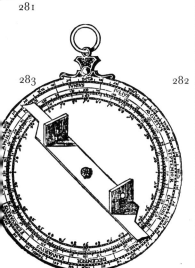

283

282

The quadrant was another of the basic instruments of navigation which remained in constant use from the earliest times until it was replaced by the sextant. A quadrant is a quarter of a circle, with a scale reading from 1° to 90° marked on the curved edge, and two pinhole sights along one of the straight edges. A plumb line is hung from the apex or point. The sights are aligned on the star under observation, and the reading is taken from the point where the plumb line touches the scale. Its main disadvantage was that when a ship pitched, the plumb line would swing. This naturally made an accurate reading very difficult to take. Shown here is a fifteenth-century Davis' quadrant (285) and, for comparison, a much more modern sextant (287). The compass, introduced into Europe in the

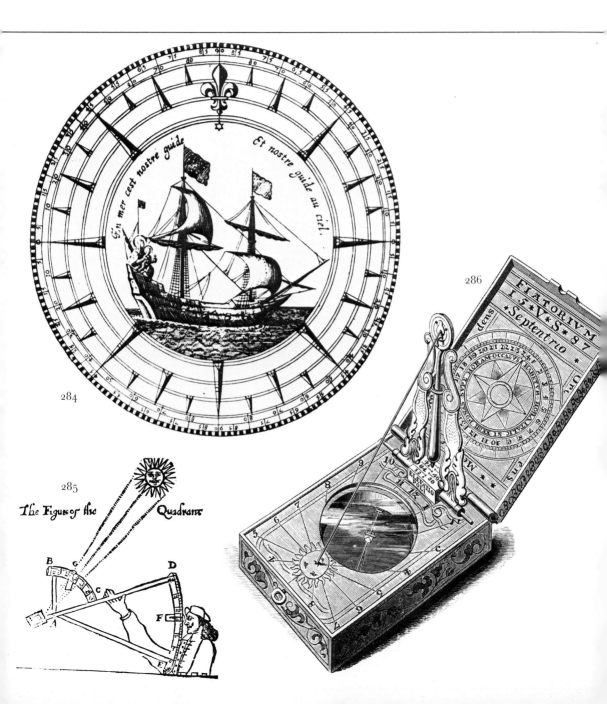

284

286

285

The Figure of the   Quadrant

thirteenth century, was not particularly useful until magnetic variation was realized and understood. Figure (286) shows a journey ring, or *viatorium*, of 1587, and (289) a box for taking compass bearings, at the beginning of the seventeenth century. The compass rose rotates on a pivot inside the box. Figure (284) shows a compass rose made in 1643, divided into thirty-two points—not degrees—and (288) a celestial globe from a treatise by the famous astronomer Tycho Brahe. This globe is five feet in diameter. Astronomy helped navigation enormously in the age of discovery, and in fact much of the science of navigation was adapted from terrestrial astronomy. The globe is decorated with signs of the Zodiac, including Scorpio, Leo, Taurus, Gemini and others.

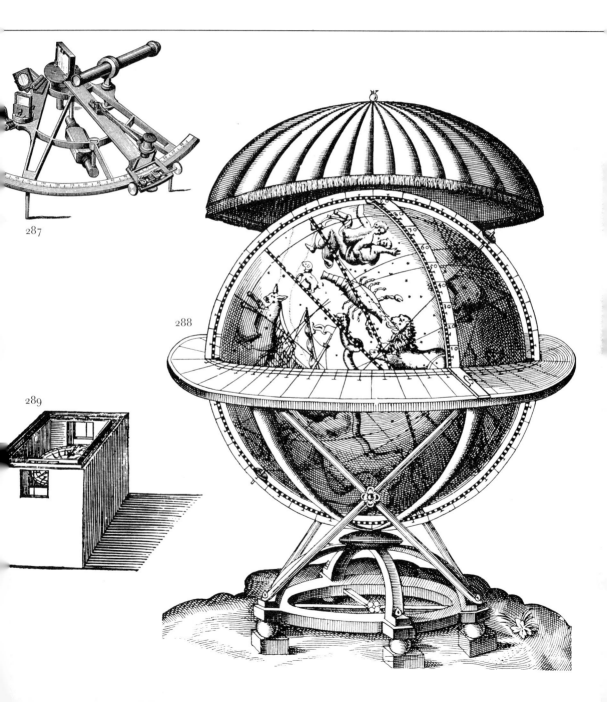

287

288

289

Figure (290) shows an Italian mariner's compass, dated 1580, in an ivory case; figure (291) shows an azimuth arc of the heavens compass of about 1785. The arc taken was that from the zenith directly above, to the edge of the horizon. Cook used azimuth compasses on all three of his voyages and, in particular, a type developed by Dr. Gowin Knight. Note the brass gimbals, which keep the compass level. Brass is chosen because the metal is not affected by a magnetic field. Figure (292) is a Hadley's sextant, and (293) Kendall's third marine chronometer, as used by Cook in *Discovery* on his third voyage. Chronometers are timekeepers of exceptional accuracy, used originally in navigation. John Harrison (1693–1776) perfected the first by introducing the principle of compensating for the expansion and contraction of the metals used in clock making. The Admiralty offered a financial

290

291

reward to the maker of the most accurate chronometer, and, although Harrison had clearly carried the day, the Admiralty was extremely reluctant to pay him. Eventually they gave him part of the money but did not pay the balance until he had proved that the results of the chronometer test were not simply a freak. After this, Kendall produced an exact copy of Harrison's fourth chronometer, which Cook took with him on his second voyage and referred to as "our trusty friend." Figure (294) is Harrison's chronometer, and (295) shows Kendall's copy. Figure (296) shows a Hadley's octant of 1827, made of copper with a reversible screw, a magnifying glass, and astronomical mirror, and (299) is a Borda's reflection instrument, invented in 1775. This improved model dates from 1827. Figures (297, 298) show relics of the Franklin expedition, including a chronometer and sextant.

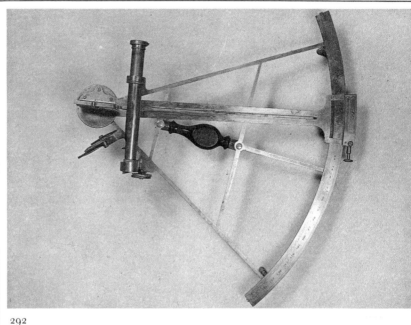

292

293

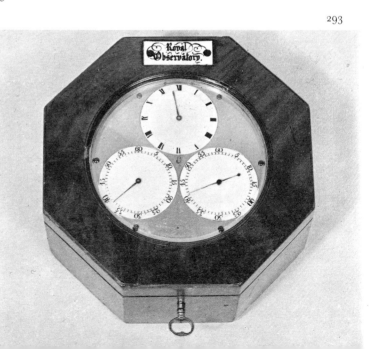

294

295

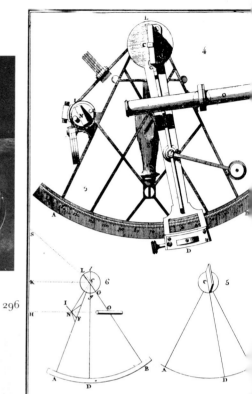

296

297

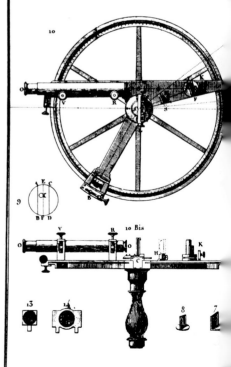

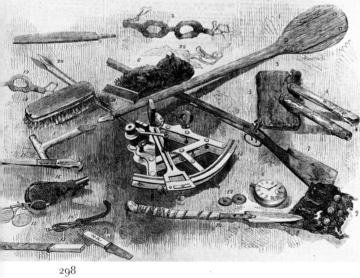

298

299

PICTURE CREDITS

The Publishers wish to express their gratitude to the following for permission to reproduce the following illustrations: The Radio Times Hulton Picture Library, 1, 10, 25, 27, 30, 38, 40, 41, 46, 52, 56, 58, 76, 77, 78, 82, 110, 118, 129, 134, 145, 146, 149, 175, 176, 177, 178, 181, 197, 198, 199, 200, 201, 202, 207, 210, 211, 212, 213, 222, 223, 225, 226, 246, 250, 259, 280, 294, 295, 297, 298; The Michael Holford Library, 3, 4, 6, 13, 32, 34, 35, 37, 51, 125, 290, 291, 292, 293; The Mansell Collection, 2, 5, 8, 9, 11, 12, 14, 15, 16, 17, 18, 19, 20, 21, 22, 23, 24, 36, 42, 45, 55, 57, 74, 127, 132, 133, 137, 219, 228, 265, 277; The Portuguese State Tourist Office, 44, 47, 70; The Trustees of the National Maritime Museum, 50, 104, 111, 116, 124, 148, 151, 152, 153, 163, 165, 166, 174, 196, 206, 208, 231, 235, 238, 267, 278; The Trustees of the British Museum, 54, 73; John Freeman & Co., 282; The Trustees of the Science Museum, 281; The Trustees of the National Portrait Gallery, 141, 256; The Weaver-Smith Collection, 150, 233, 237, 249, 266, 272, 276; Paul Popper Ltd., 254; Picture Point Ltd., 229, 230, 239, 240, 241, 242, 243, 244. Other illustrations appearing in this book are the property of The Wayland Picture Library.

FURTHER READING

CONTEMPORARY ACCOUNTS

Marco Polo: The description of the World, edited and translated by A. C. Moule and
    P. Pelliot (London, 1938)
Mandeville's Travels, edited by M. Letts, 2 vols (London, 1953)
The Journal of Christopher Columbus, translated by C. Jane and revised and annotated by
    L. A. Vigneras (London, 1960)
A Journal of the first voyage of Vasco da Gama, edited by E. G. Ravenstein (London, 1898)
The Voyages of Martin Frobisher, edited by R. Collinson (London, 1889)
Cook's first voyage, round the Horn and the Cape of Good Hope, 1768–71, was
    compiled by J. Hawkesworth from the journals of Cook and Banks, and first published
    in 1773. Cook's own *Journal* was edited by Wharton in 1893.
A Voyage towards the South Pole and round the World in 1772–5, James Cook (London, 1777)
A Voyage to the Pacific Ocean in 1776–80, James Cook (London, 1784). The third volume
    by Captain T. King. Available in Everyman Edition
A Voyage of Discovery made for the purpose of exploring Baffin Bay, John Ross (London, 1819)
Journal of a Voyage for the Discovery of a North-West Passage from the Atlantic to the Pacific,
    W. E. Parry (London, 1821)
Narrative of the Exploring Expedition, by Authority of Congress, during the years 1838–1842,
    Charles Wilkes (Philadelphia, 1845)
A Voyage of Discovery and Research in the Southern and Antarctic Regions, James Clark Ross
    (London, 1847)
The Voyage of the Discovery, R. F. Scott (London, 1905)
South Pole, R. Amundsen (London, 1912)

MODERN WORKS

Baker, J. N. L., *A history of geographical discovery and exploration* (London, 1937)
Beaglehole, J. C., *The exploration of the Pacific* (London, 1934)
Brown, L. A., *The Story of Maps* (Boston, 1950)
Caras, R. A., *Antarctica: Land of Frozen Time* (Philadelphia and New York, 1962)
Clowes, G. S. L., *Sailing ships: their history and development* (London, 1931–6)
Hart, H. H., *Sea Road to the Indies* (New York, 1950)
Heawood, E., *A history of geographical discovery in the seventeenth and eighteenth centuries*
    (London, 1912)
Mirsky, J., *To the Arctic* (New York, 1948)
Morison, S. E., *Admiral of the Ocean Sea* (Boston, 1942)
Newton, A. P. (ed.), *Travel and travellers of the Middle Ages* (London, 1930)

INDEX